Be
Not
Deceived

How to Know the Truth

According to the Scriptures

J. Phillips

Free printable Bible study and eBook versions are available at:
www.ABetterBibleStudyMethod.com

Be Not Deceived, A Better Bible Study Method – Book Two
© 2017 by J. Phillips

Free eBook and free printable Bible study versions available at:
www.ABetterBibleStudyMethod.com

Send all correspondence to:
ABetterBibleStudyMethod.com
PO Box 885, Lockport, IL 60441
Phone: (770) 842-6370

ISBN13: 978-0-9702687-7-8
Library of Congress Control Number: 2015900356

All rights reserved. To promote Bible study, copies may be printed in any language if they contain the complete, unaltered text of this book and are not sold for profit. Those who want to reprint this book or to translate it into a foreign language can contact us for electronic files that can be used for this purpose. Any excerpts from or uses of this material must cite or link to ABetterBibleStudyMethod.com and all electronic excerpts are limited to 200 words.

All scripture references are from the Holy Bible, King James Version.

Be Not Deceived

Table of Contents

Preface

"Whom the LORD loveth he correcteth" (Prv 3:12).

"Reproofs of instruction *are* the way of life" (Prv 6:23).

"The fear of the LORD *is* a fountain of life" (Prv 14:27).

"Teach me thy way, O LORD; I will walk in thy truth" (Ps 86:11).

"O LORD: give me understanding according to thy word" (Ps 119:169).

"The fear of the LORD *is* the instruction of wisdom; and before honor *is* humility" (Prv 15:33).

"Give unto the LORD the glory due unto his name" (Ps 96:8).

"Thou hast magnified thy word above all thy name" (Ps 138:2).

"The word of our God shall stand for ever" (Is 40:8).

"Thy word *is* a lamp unto my feet, and a light unto my path" (Ps 119:105).

"The entrance of thy words giveth light" (Ps 119:130).

"All scripture *is* given by inspiration of God" (2 Tm 3:16).

"He that is faithful in that which is least is faithful also in much: and he that is unjust in the least is unjust also in much" (Lk 16:10).

"A little leaven leaveneth the whole lump" (Gal 5:9).

"Cease, my son, to hear the instruction *that causeth* to err from the words of knowledge" (Prv 19:27).

"Wherewithal shall a young man cleanse his way? by taking heed *thereto* according to thy word" (Ps 119:9).

"The fear of man bringeth a snare: but whoso putteth his trust in the LORD shall be safe" (Prv 29:25).

"The fear of the LORD *is* the beginning of wisdom" (Ps 111:10).

"The LORD *is* nigh unto all them that call upon him, to all that call upon him in truth" (Ps 145:18).

Introduction

How should we go about determining what is true on biblical matters? We should do so according to the scriptures. Proverbs 30:5 tells us, **"Every word of God** *is* pure: he *is* a shield unto them that put their trust in him,"** and the evidence herein will show how God's word can correct errors in our understanding or prevent them from occurring in the first place. For instance, the following example shows how terms used in scripture can be easily misunderstood if they are not defined according to a biblical standard.

Word pictures, or figures of speech, are used in language to briefly convey a complex idea. A word picture that was used several times by Jesus was that of drinking a man's blood, such as when he said, "Whoso eateth my flesh, and drinketh my blood, hath eternal life; and I will raise him up at the last day" (Fourth gospel 6:54). Given his words, should one assume drinking his blood referred to sipping the liquid in his veins? No, to do so would only reveal a problem with the method that was used by anyone who comes to such a conclusion.

On other occasions the Jews picked up stones to stone Jesus or they tried to throw him off a cliff (cf. Lu 4:29, Fourth gospel 8:59, 10:31). Yet, they did not react this way when Jesus said, "Whoso eateth my flesh, and drinketh my blood, hath eternal life." Why not? Because God's word had already established what his words meant.

Consider the following example from the life of David that shows how a straightforward reading of scripture can open our eyes to the truth like nothing else can. This took place when David was in "the cave of Adullam" (1 Chr 11:15), the city of Bethlehem was in Philistine hands, and three of David's "mighty men" (cf. 2 Samuel 23:16-17) risked their lives on a covert mission behind enemy lines:

> "David *was* then in the hold, and the Philistines' garrison *was* then at Bethlehem. And David longed, and said, Oh that one would give me drink of the water of the well of Bethlehem, that *is* at the gate! And the three brake through the host of the Philistines, and drew water out of the well of Bethlehem, that *was* by the gate, and took *it*, and brought *it* to David: but David would not drink *of* it, but poured it out to the LORD, And said, My God forbid it me, that I should do this thing: shall I drink the blood of these men that have put their lives in jeopardy? For with *the jeopardy of* their lives they brought it. **Therefore he would not drink it**" (1 Chr 11:16-19).

When "the three" brought the water to David, he refused to drink it! Some might think David's response to their gift would have shocked or even infuriated the men who put their lives in jeopardy in order to get it. However, if he did right in the sight of the LORD when he "would not drink of it, but poured it out to the LORD," then his act provided an important lesson about the value of life to those three men, along with the rest of David's men and all the readers of scripture since then.

In any case, "the well of Bethlehem" passage does more than provide a record of those events for people who read the Bible today. It also gives us the key to a word picture that is found elsewhere in scripture. When a person learns how this works, then that person learns one of the ways the Bible can teach people how to separate truth from error.

The way to understand the things in God's word is to consider them in light of the whole counsel of God. When David poured out the water "to the LORD" he said, "shall I drink the blood of these men that have put their lives in jeopardy?" (1 Chr 11:19). "Drink the blood" was, clearly, not a physical description. Rather, it is a word picture about one man accepting the sacrifice of another man's life on his behalf – and this is precisely how people need to view themselves in relation to Jesus!

Why would anyone teach about the blood of Jesus and fail to mention the foregoing point if scripture itself can establish a clear connection?

Jesus' statements, "Whoso eateth my flesh, and drinketh my blood, hath eternal life; and I will raise him up at the last day," and "He that eateth my flesh, and drinketh my blood, dwelleth in me, and I in him" (Fourth gospel 6:54 & 56), displeased some of his disciples. We know this because the passage that records those words is followed by a note that says "many" of his disciples called Jesus' words a "hard saying" and they "murmured at it" (Fourth gospel 6:60-61).

If they knew about David's use of this word picture, then why did they kick against Jesus' words?

It is a natural response for those who do not think eternal life depends on Jesus laying down his life on their behalf, and later we will consider how pride sometimes leads people to resist truth to their own hurt.

The wisdom of the world leads some to think Jesus' use of the phrase "drinketh my blood" means eternal life depends on the oral intake of a liquid (his blood), yet this is not true. In the two "well of Bethlehem" passages (2 Sa 23:14-17, 1 Chr 11:16-19), **God's word provides the key to the word picture that was used by Jesus** (and it always has).

People can see this and think it through once scripture teaches them to see "drink the blood" as a word picture. Until this occurs, however, a lack of knowledge leads many to be deceived as they misconstrue those words and go on to attribute a wrong meaning to Jesus' words. In the same way, we end up deceived when a wrong assumption or an erroneous teaching leads us to think an idea is true when it is not.

As the above example showed, we must view the words **of** scripture according **to** scripture or we get it wrong; and this book will show how upholding God's word as the measure of truth on biblical issues can counteract the effects of false assumptions and unbiblical methods.

"Be not deceived" is a warning that shows up in several Bible verses. Those verses, along with many others, let us know followers of Jesus can be misled. But the words "be not deceived" also indicate people can take steps to keep this from happening. Honoring God's word is one of those steps and yet, as the Bible reveals, sometimes people choose to honor the teachings of men instead.

Jesus publicly berated the religious leaders of his day who promoted the teachings of men, instead of faithfully speaking the word of God. He said:

"Esaias prophesied of you hypocrites, as it is written, This people honoreth me with *their* lips, but their heart is far from me. Howbeit in vain do they worship me, teaching *for* doctrines the commandments of men. For laying aside the commandment of God, ye hold the tradition of men" (Mk 7:6-8).

Their preference for the teachings of men is what led them to trample on the authority of God, as Jesus noted when he said: "Ye reject the commandment of God, that ye may keep your own tradition" (Mk 7:9) and when he said they were "making the word of God of none effect" through their tradition (Mk 7:13).

At another time, Jesus said, "Woe unto you, scribes and Pharisees, hypocrites! for ye compass sea and land to make one proselyte, and when he is made, ye make him twofold more the child of hell than yourselves" (Mt 23:15). He did not rebuke those missionaries for their missionary zeal, but because they did not lead people to trust in God. Rather, they produced converts who would follow them in trusting in the teachings of men (i.e., adopt their belief system; join their group).

"*It is* better to trust in the LORD than to put confidence in man" (Ps 118:8). Since this is true, scripture will be the only source cited herein.

If we can make mistakes, it makes sense to test our beliefs and invite biblical correction. Conversely, it makes no sense to turn a blind eye to scripture on any point, for if we disregard the truth on one issue, then we are taking a pick and choose approach to God's word.

If our Bible study method leads us to hold a wrong view on one issue, then it may have done so on other matters. This is why it is important to focus on the process we use to go about ascertaining biblical truth.

Whenever we learn our view on a verse or issue was wrong, we need to ask ourselves, *'What caused me to be deceived on this – where is the flaw in my method of assessing truth?'* Identifying the source of a problem allows us to take steps to improve our Bible study method. Asking good questions is critical to the pursuit of truth and this book will show how scripture can draw us to the truth by raising questions that provoke us to search for an answer. Looking for and pondering the questions that the word of God presents to us is a key element of a better Bible study method. So, when you find a question in this book that helps you to see things in scripture which you did not see before, then consider that example and take note of how the facts in scripture can teach us by raising a question that demands a biblical answer.

Many people think a good way of deciding what to believe is to pick a view which is *'traditional'* or is espoused by one or more scholars. However, scripture tells us this practice is not wise, as will be shown.

[Note: herein a number of commonly taught ideas will be shown to be contrary to scripture. Any readers of this book who are not aware of some of these ideas can easily confirm if an idea is commonly taught by doing a simple Internet search on the topic or verse in question. Also, this book cannot deal with every element in all of the passages that will be considered. Nevertheless, a truth that is confirmed by the biblical evidence on any point needs to be respected, even if one still has other unanswered questions that are related to the same issue.]

Results speak for themselves, so the case studies herein will contrast the results of the common practice of relying on the teachings of men with the results of sticking to an evidence-based Bible study method. If one of those methods honors God's authority and can consistently produce better results, then the contrast will make this apparent.

A high regard for the name of the LORD is encouraged in scripture, as we see in these words, "Our Father which art in heaven, Hallowed be thy name" (Mt 6:9, Lk 11:2). But Psalm 138:2 also tells us this about the LORD, "thou has magnified thy word **above** all thy name." So, one should be diligent to always have the highest regard for his word.

Chapter 1 – "Founded Upon a Rock"

"The fear of the LORD *is* the beginning of knowledge" (Prv 1:7).

<u>"Trust in the LORD"</u>

This chapter looks at some principles for a better Bible study method – starting with "Trust in the LORD with all thine heart; and lean not unto thine own understanding. In all thy ways acknowledge him, and he shall direct thy paths" (Prv 3:5-6). Along with every other admonition in the Bible, those words should influence one's approach to scripture (because the counsel that is in the word of God also teaches us how to rightly divide God's word).

The words "Trust in the LORD with all thine heart; and lean not unto thine own understanding" contrast the source of truth with a person's current views and assumptions. Whenever we let our understanding serve as our measure of truth, we are not trusting in the LORD with all our heart. So, we need to be diligent about obeying this passage.

"Lean not unto thine own understanding" does not mean we should lean on the understanding of other men. If other men should not lean on their own understanding, then we cannot assume it is safe for us to rely on their understanding! The passage then says, "In all thy ways **acknowledge him**, and he shall direct thy paths," and the examples in this book show how God's word works to lead people to the truth.

<u>Profiting from Biblical Correction</u>

Paul urged Timothy to strive to be "a workman that needeth not to be ashamed, rightly dividing the word of truth" (2 Tm 2:15). "Rightly dividing the word of truth" takes diligence, but it also takes humility, because we have to stand corrected when God's word shows us we have been wrong about something.

"All scripture *is* given by inspiration of God, and *is* profitable for doctrine, for reproof, for correction, for instruction in righteousness" (2 Tm 3:16). Profiting from scripture comes at a cost. If we want to profit when it comes to "doctrine," "reproof," "correction," or "instruction," something must change. While it is easy to say we want to *'go deeper in God's word'* or to *'grow in grace and knowledge,'* two things are true:

(A) there is no such thing as growth without change, and
(B) change often makes people uncomfortable, which can lead people to resist change for this reason alone.

If we find out something we believed is not in line with God's word and subsequently change our thinking to be in accord with scripture, then that would be an example of "correction." This cannot happen unless we are willing to admit we have been wrong. Yet, no one likes having their judgment called into question. This is why we need to be conscious of the tug of war which goes on between pride and humility (because pride naturally tends to lead us to resist correction).

"God resisteth the proud, and giveth grace to the humble" (1 Pt 5:5), so if we want "grace," humility is a good first step. We will come back to this verse in a minute. For now, though, realize we have to admit we have been wrong in order to profit from biblical correction, and this humbling process can also help us to receive the grace of God.

Many people have had the experience of reading a verse and getting a new insight that corrects their understanding. In such moments, a key benefit of biblical correction is lost if we do not realize correction teaches us more than just the truth on a particular issue.

<u>Correction on Two Fronts</u>

A common saying tells us giving a man a fish helps him for a day, but teaching him how to fish helps him even more. This idea can help us to see the two different ways we can benefit from biblical correction. Learning the truth on any issue is good. If we stop there, however, it is like taking the fish and skipping the fishing lesson.

A teacher can give a student the answer to a math question. But to help the student grow, the teacher needs to show the student how to derive the answer. Biblical correction can do both! God's word can move us from error to truth on a given issue, and it can also teach us how to rightly derive the answer. This is why we can profit more from biblical correction if we identify what caused us to be deceived when it turns out we have believed something that was not true.

This book does not merely put a new spin on certain verses. Rather, it will show how unbiblical methods cause people to be deceived, and it will also show how God's word provides us a reliable measure for discerning truth on biblical issues.

Jesus told his followers, "Take heed what ye hear: with what measure ye mete, it shall be measured to you" (Mk 4:24). This indicates we must be careful when it comes to what we hear because <u>what we "hear" affects the "measure" we use, and the measure we use affects how we perceive things</u>.

If we believe what we hear, then that becomes part of the measure we use when we are deciding what is true. If something we believe is actually not true, then that false belief will lead us to be deceived on other matters.

"The Wisdom of this World"

"Let no man deceive himself. If any man among you seemeth to be wise in this world, let him become a fool, that he may be wise. For the wisdom of this world is foolishness with God" (1 Cor 3:18-19). The words "let no man deceive himself" were written "to them that are sanctified in Christ Jesus" (1 Cor 1:2), so we should not think believers today are impervious to being deceived.

If scripture says, "the wisdom of this world is foolishness with God," we should realize people who apply worldly wisdom to their study of God's word are likely to be led astray. This question, "hath not God made foolish the wisdom of this world?" (1 Cor 1:20) and this statement, "God hath chosen the foolish things of the world to confound the wise; and God hath chosen the weak things of the world to confound the things which are mighty" (1 Cor 1:27) suggest the same thing. But sadly, "the wisdom of this world" is the foundation which underlies many of the ideas which are presented as biblical truth in our day.

The public is taught to esteem men with degrees and titles. Yet men with the same status or level of training often contradict each other. So, the honors men bestow upon other men offer *no* guarantee that the truth will always be taught by the ones who receive such honors. This is why we need to subject every teaching to biblical scrutiny.

"Measuring Themselves by Themselves"

It goes against the advice of scripture, but measuring truth by looking at what others believe is a common practice. In 2 Corinthians 10:12, Paul and Timothy wrote, "we dare not make ourselves of the number, or compare ourselves with some that commend themselves: but they measuring themselves by themselves, and comparing themselves among themselves, are not wise." Thus, looking to what others think and conforming our mind to some groupthink measure is not a wise thing to do. Nevertheless, people today are often urged to assume 'the consensus' is where the truth lies.

If the beliefs of men and popular ideas (i.e., 'the consensus') are not good ways to measure the truth, then what measure should we use? We should look to scripture as the standard of truth on biblical issues.

Acts 17:11 tells us the Bereans "received the word with all readiness of mind, and searched the scriptures daily, whether those things were so," and this offers us a good model.

A good investigator does not base his conclusions on the conclusions of others. Instead he will base his conclusions on the evidence, and when we are considering biblical issues, our conclusions should be dictated by the evidence in scripture. Being driven to a conclusion on a biblical issue because of what is said in God's word is not the same as holding a belief because others hold that belief. Still many simply adopt the beliefs that are taught to them and assume those ideas are in line with scripture. But if we trust *what people say about scripture* before we look to scripture itself, are we honoring God by doing so?

If someone says the Bible says 'x,' how would you know if that is true or not? Often people say *'the Bible says...'* and then state their beliefs on an issue. No doubt they do so because they assume their beliefs are true, but what if they are wrong? What test can a person use to know if someone has misconstrued or misrepresented God's word? God's word is the authority on biblical issues. If we let the authority of non-Bible sources serve as our measure of truth, then the authority of God's word is undermined. If we want to know what is scriptural, we need to use scripture as our measure. Period!

"Written for Our Learning"

Jesus frequently confronted those who substituted their own ideas and teachings for the truth found in God's word and a few of those exchanges will be cited to show how we can learn from the correction Jesus offered them. In Jesus' day the only scripture they had was the portion of the Bible which we call the Old Testament. Some think the Old Testament has little to say to the followers of Jesus. However, the New Testament lets us know this is not the case.

1 Corinthians 10:11 says, "Now all these things happened unto them for examples and they are written for our admonition." Romans 15:4 says, "Whatsoever things were written aforetime were written for our learning." So, the followers of Jesus can learn from the things written in the Old Testament. For example, consider what we can learn from this report about Naaman the leper from 2 Kings 5:1 & 9-14:

> "Naaman, captain of the host of the king of Syria, was a great man with his master and honorable, because by him the LORD had given deliverance unto Syria: he was also a mighty man in valor, *but he was* a leper... Naaman came with his horses and with his chariot, and stood at the door of the house of Elisha.

And Elisha sent a messenger unto him, saying, Go and wash in Jordan seven times, and thy flesh shall come again to thee, and thou shalt be clean. But Naaman was wroth, and went away, and said, Behold, I thought, He will surely come out to me, and stand, and call on the name of the LORD his God, and strike his hand over the place, and recover the leper. *Are* not Abana and Pharpar, rivers of Damascus, better than all the waters of Israel? May I not wash in them, and be clean? So he turned and went away in a rage. And his servants came near, and spake unto him, and said, My father, *if* the prophet had bid thee *do some* great thing, wouldest thou not have done *it?* How much rather then, when he saith to thee, Wash, and be clean? Then went he down, and dipped himself seven times in Jordan, according to the saying of the man of God: and his flesh came again like unto the flesh of a little child, and he was clean."

What strikes you from the foregoing account? A Bible passage can teach many things, but one of the most striking things in this passage has to be Naaman's near-miss. First he turned away from the truth the messenger had delivered. Then he obeyed, and he was healed as a result. What can we learn from this episode?

How to Get Grace

"God resisteth the proud, and giveth grace to the humble" (1 Pt 5:5). The contrast in this verse shows how the choices people make can affect their relationship with God. At one point, Naaman was on the wrong side of that formula, and the benefit of a humble response to the truth is highlighted by what happened after he humbled himself.

Naaman was a key man in his country, but he had leprosy. He heard of a prophet in Samaria who could help him recover and his pursuit of a healing led him to Elisha's house. Naaman arrived "with his horses and with his chariot" and, no doubt, an entourage befitting a man of his status, which explains the presence of "his servants." We are told, he "stood at the door of the house of Elisha." Scripture does not say how long he stood there, so we cannot tell if he had to wait a while or if he got a fast response. What it does say, however, lets us know Naaman was not happy with the way things transpired.

Elisha did not come out to greet Naaman. He "sent a messenger unto him." The messenger told Naaman, "Go and wash in Jordan seven times, and thy flesh shall come again to thee and thou shalt be clean." Naaman did not say thank you or rush off to wash to see if it worked. Instead, "Naaman was wroth, and went away."

Clearly, Elisha's communication via a messenger and his prescription for healing did not fit Naaman's view of what should have happened:

> "I thought, He will surely come out to me, and stand, and call on the name of the LORD his God, and strike his hand over the place, and recover the leper. *Are* not Abana and Pharpar, rivers of Damascus, better than all the waters of Israel? May I not wash in them, and be clean? So he turned and went away in a rage" (2 Kgs 5:11-12).

At that point Naaman, leaning on his own understanding, decided he knew better than the word which was spoken by Elisha's messenger. Does this, along with his anger and his boast of "better" rivers in his own country, indicate pride was what led him to storm off in a rage? If so, then we need to consider the episode in light of this verse: "God resisteth the proud, and giveth grace to the humble."

Sound Reasoning Exposes Unreasonable Thinking

What was the result of Naaman's decision to reject the truth that was presented by the messenger? It brought him no blessing. Contrast this with the result of his later decision to submit to the logic that was used to prove he was not being reasonable. "His servants came near, and spake unto him, and said, My father, *if* the prophet had bid thee *do some* great thing wouldest thou not have done *it*? how much rather then, when he saith to thee, Wash, and be clean?"

"Wash in Jordan seven times, and thy flesh shall come again to thee, and thou shalt be clean" was a promise of healing, so it made sense to try it. It was unreasonable to ignore the message simply because it was delivered by a messenger and/or it did not conform to his view of what was "better."

Elisha's reputation brought Naaman to his door. Still, Naaman did not believe the promise, for if he had, his desire to be healed would have led him to obey. Because the promise came via a messenger and/or because Naaman did not like the prescribed remedy, he concluded the offer in those words did not deserve respect. However, when his servants presented a logical argument that proved he was not being reasonable, his humbling response to their correction enabled him to receive the blessing those words had promised all along.

Since the servants' question showed he was being unreasonable, he could have become angry or defensive. Yet, rather than turn on them because they had questioned his judgment, he submitted to the truth.

He did the same thing we need to do whenever we have been wrong or unreasonable. He exhibited humility. He set aside his pride and admitted he had been wrong.

The Authority of the Message

Elisha was not the authority behind the message. When Elisha spoke a truth from God, his words carried God's authority. This same idea is echoed in these words written to the church of the Thessalonians: "For this cause also thank we God without ceasing, because, when ye received the word of God which ye heard of us, ye received *it* not *as* the word of men, but as it is in truth, the word of God" (1 Th 2:13). Although the Thessalonians heard words that were spoken by men, they did not receive them as merely being "the word of men." Just the opposite, they rightly "received" the message as "the word of God."

Naaman did not receive the message as it was "in truth" until he faced an argument showing his position could not stand the test of reason. In the same way, if we learn a belief of ours is contrary to scripture, then we must stand corrected. The admonition, "Today if ye will hear his voice, harden not your hearts" (Ps 95:7-8) warns against resisting the truth, and if the things in scripture were "written for our learning" (Rom 15:4), then we need to heed those words.

Treating God's Word with Respect

"The truth shall make you free" is a commonly quoted line that distorts the words of Jesus. Integrity should lead us to consider his words in light of the context where they appear. The truth is those words were addressed to people who "believed on him," and those words are only the last part of a qualified statement: "If **ye** continue in my word, *then* are **ye** my disciples indeed; and **ye** shall know the truth, and the truth shall make **you** free" (Fourth gospel 8:31-32).

"If ye continue in my word" is a condition. Thus, it is wrong to treat the words, "the truth shall make you free" as if they were a promise to all people even if they do not believe on Jesus or "continue in" his word. While it may tickle the ears of an audience, quoting "the truth shall make you free" without any conditions falsely represents God's word (by taking away the conditions which precede those words).

Taking a verse out of context is something preachers will frequently speak against, and this is good. However, if those who deride others for taking verses out of context do the same thing at certain points in their own teaching, then they are being <u>inconsistent</u>.

Even if it is not done intentionally, God's word is misrepresented when scripture is misquoted. This is why it is important for us to be diligent to speak the word of God faithfully (cf. Jer 23:28).

The Case Studies

The only authority cited herein is God's word. Scripture will be used to test some common views on a given Bible passage. If those views cannot hold up under biblical scrutiny, then we can benefit by learning what led others to miss the truth on those points. So, various methods of assessing truth on biblical issues will also be considered. You can also put your own method to the test in each case. It may be that the evidence will challenge your own views on various points. But, if we want to avoid leaning on our "own understanding," then we should be willing to make sure our own beliefs can stand up to biblical scrutiny.

The King James Version is used herein, so you may occasionally find an unfamiliar word or spelling. Those who use other Bible translations can still follow the biblical evidence and it will make the same points.

Note: since scripture is the only source quoted in this book, <u>the use of double quotation marks will be reserved for quotes from scripture</u>. Single quotation marks will, therefore, be used in other places where double quotation marks would traditionally appear. Also, when words in a Bible quote appear in italics, it is because this is how those words appear in the KJV.

"A Lamp unto My Feet"

"Thy word *is* a lamp unto my feet, and a light unto my path" (Ps 119:105). This verse pictures one of the ways the word of God can direct us if we will let it show us where to stand on an issue and where to go with a thought. As will be shown, if we let God's word light the way as we move through scripture, it can focus our attention on things we might otherwise miss. But if scripture teaches us something, then we have an obligation to act on that information.

Jesus compared those who hear his sayings and act accordingly to a "wise man" who built a house that can stand up to storms because it was "founded upon a rock" (Mt 7:24-25). Then he likened those who hear his sayings but do not act accordingly to a "foolish" man who built a house that would fall in a storm because it was built "on sand" (Mt 7:26-27). Similarly, if scripture teaches us something and thereafter we do not act in accord with what we have learned, then we are being unreasonable and making the word of God of no effect.

Chapter 2 – The Case of David's Turn

<u>A Turning Away from God</u>

One of the most famous episodes in the Bible is the adulterous affair between David and the wife of Uriah the Hittite (and those details are found in 2 Samuel, starting in 11:1 and continuing through 12:15). You can put your Bible study method to the test by doing what you would normally do when you consider a passage. Set this book aside and get your Bible. Read 2 Samuel 11:1-12:15 and any other relevant verses, then jot down your thoughts about this passage of scripture.

Then consider the biblical evidence this case study presents and see if the evidence-based method modeled herein would help you to get better results.

###

The Case of David's Turn

David

The prominence of David is made clear in a number of Bible verses. For example, the opening of the book of Matthew says, "The book of the generation of Jesus Christ, the son of David, the son of Abraham" (Mt 1:1). In this verse David is singled out with Abraham as an ancestor in the line of Jesus.

When the prophet Samuel gave the following rebuke to king Saul, his words included a striking compliment regarding the man who would replace Saul (i.e., David) – "But now thy kingdom shall not continue: the LORD hath sought him <u>a man after his own heart</u>, and the LORD hath commanded him *to be* captain over his people" (1 Sa 13:14). In his address to the men of Israel in Acts 13, this compliment was cited by the apostle Paul when he linked David to Jesus:

> "He [God] raised up unto them David to be their king; to whom also he gave testimony, and said, I have found David the *son* of Jesse, a man after mine own heart, which shall fulfill all my will. Of this man's seed hath God according to *his* promise raised unto Israel a Savior, Jesus" (Acts 13:22-23).

Those verses are where we are told about David being a man after God's own heart. In contrast 1 Kings 15:5 says, "David did *that which was* right in the eyes of the LORD, and turned not aside from any *thing* that he commanded him all the days of his life, save only in the matter of Uriah the Hittite." Those words might well bring to mind the time when David numbered the people and seventy thousand men died as a result (cf. 2 Sa 24:1-15, 1 Chr 21:1-14), or other episodes in his life. Still, unlike any other thing, "the matter of Uriah the Hittite" is singled out as the only time when David turned aside from something the LORD commanded him. This should arrest our attention. (It also teaches us that in the sight of the LORD "the matter of Uriah the Hittite" is different from all the other things David did that were less than ideal.)

David Takes Uriah's Wife

2 Samuel 11:1-5 is the only place where scripture records David's adulterous affair with the wife of Uriah the Hittite:

> "And it came to pass, after the year was expired, at the time when kings go forth *to battle*, that David sent Joab, and his servants with him, and all Israel; and they destroyed the

children of Ammon, and besieged Rabbah. But David tarried still at Jerusalem. And it came to pass in an evening, that David arose from off his bed, and walked upon the roof of the king's house: and from the roof he saw a woman washing herself; and the woman *was* very beautiful to look upon. And David sent and enquired after the woman. And *one* said, *Is* not this Bathsheba, the daughter of Eliam, the wife of Uriah the Hittite? And David sent messengers, and took her; and she came in unto him, and he lay with her; for she was purified from her uncleanness: and she returned unto her house. And the woman conceived, and sent and told David, and said, I *am* with child."

Notice what occurred as David acted on his lustful thoughts. When "David sent and enquired after the woman" scripture notes this: "And *one* said, *Is* not this Bathsheba, the daughter of Eliam, the wife of Uriah the Hittite?" A superficial look at those verses may lead some people to assume "enquired after the woman" means David asked about the identity of a beautiful stranger. This would, in turn, tend to lead one to see the statement about "the daughter of Eliam, the wife of Uriah the Hittite" as being nothing more than a report about the identity of the woman (in response to his inquiry).

Yet, it turns out there are details in scripture that indicate the words "*Is* not this Bathsheba, the daughter of Eliam, the wife of Uriah the Hittite" may have been a rebuke to David, and not merely an answer to a question about the woman's identity. Even if those words were not a rebuke, the evidence will show scripture is not simply describing an adulterous union that followed a momentary lapse of judgment on the part of David. What he did was far, far worse.

David and Uriah

After "the woman conceived, and sent and told David, and said, I *am* with child" (2 Sa 11:5), the plot thickened as David schemed to avoid having to deal with the awkward result of his affair with Uriah's wife. This is what happened next:

"And David sent to Joab, *saying*, Send me Uriah the Hittite. And Joab sent Uriah to David. And when Uriah was come unto him, David demanded *of him* how Joab did, and how the people did, and how the war prospered. And David said to Uriah, Go down to thy house, and wash thy feet. And Uriah departed out of the king's house, and there followed him a mess *of meat* from the king. But Uriah slept at the door of the king's house with all the servants of his lord, and went not down to his house" (2 Sa 11:6-9).

Since Uriah was on the battlefield, people would know he was not the father of the child his wife was carrying. Clearly, David's scheme was to have the battle-weary Uriah spend the night with Bathsheba before she began to show. Then everyone, Uriah included, would mistakenly assume Uriah was the father of the child. But things did not work out the way David planned, because Uriah's affinity for his brethren who were on the battlefront moved him more than his own desires for comfort or pleasure:

> "And when they had told David, saying, Uriah went not down unto his house, David said unto Uriah, Camest thou not from *thy* journey? Why *then* didst thou not go down unto thine house? And Uriah said unto David, The ark, and Israel, and Judah, abide in tents; and my lord Joab, and the servants of my lord, are encamped in the open fields; shall I then go into mine house, to eat and to drink, and to lie with my wife? *As* thou livest and *as* thy soul liveth, I will not do this thing" (2 Sa 11:10-11).

Uriah's character deterred him from seeking his own pleasure on that night, so David came up with another plan. David told Uriah to stay in Jerusalem one more night, in the hopes of weakening Uriah's resolve by getting him drunk:

> "And David said to Uriah, Tarry here today also, and tomorrow I will let thee depart. So Uriah abode in Jerusalem that day, and the morrow. And when David had called him, he did eat and drink before him; and he made him drunk: and at evening he went out to lie on his bed with the servants of his lord, but went not down to his house" (2 Sa 11:12-13).

When his scheming proved to be no match for Uriah's integrity, David turned to desperate measures. As you will see, it may not have been fear of public embarrassment that led David to do what he did next. It could be David actually feared what this man of character might do upon learning what David had done to his wife (while he had been busy risking his life in battle on behalf of David and the nation).

David's Betrayal

David betrayed Uriah when he chose to commit adultery with his wife. Yet something convinced David that rather than risk having to face Uriah in the future, he had better get rid of him once and for all. So David arranged for Uriah to be killed in a way that would make it seem as if Uriah was a casualty of war (and leave everyone, except himself and Joab, thinking Uriah simply died an unfortunate death):

"And it came to pass in the morning, that David wrote a letter to Joab, and sent *it* by the hand of Uriah. And he wrote in the letter, saying, Set ye Uriah in the forefront of the hottest battle, and retire ye from him, that he may be smitten, and die. And it came to pass, when Joab observed the city, that he assigned Uriah unto a place where he knew that valiant men *were*. And the men of the city went out, and fought with Joab: and there fell *some* of the people of the servants of David; and Uriah the Hittite died also" (2 Sa 11:14-17).

Uriah's blood was not the only blood on David's hands, for scripture notes, "there fell *some* of the people of the servants of David; and Uriah the Hittite died also" (2 Sa 11:17). When a messenger told David what had happened, he had a very nonchalant reaction to the loss of innocent life which he has caused: "David said unto the messenger, Thus shalt thou say unto Joab, Let not this thing displease thee, for the sword devoureth one as well as another" (2 Sa 11:25).

Upon hearing about the soldiers who died as a result of his plan to get rid of Uriah, "the sword devoureth one as well as another" was David's response. Indeed, it is very sad, and very telling, that the one who was called the man after God's own heart could sink to such a low level.

<u>David Does Uriah Dirty</u>

The closing words of 2 Samuel 11 are as follows:

"And when the wife of Uriah heard that Uriah her husband was dead, she mourned for her husband. And when the mourning was past, David sent and fetched her to his house, and she became his wife, and bare him a son. But the thing that David had done displeased the LORD" (2 Sa 11:26-27).

David probably thought he had gotten away with his dastardly deeds. However, the LORD had other plans (as we will see when we consider the rebuke that was delivered to David by the prophet Nathan). Still, since David was in such a hurry to get rid of Uriah we ought to ask, Why? Should we assume fear of embarrassment over being caught in a garden-variety act of adultery was what moved David to arrange for the speedy demise of Uriah?

Given David's background, he must have known his directive to Joab would result in others being killed along with Uriah. The question is, would a fear of having his adultery exposed have been a sufficient motivation to drive David to kill Uriah and sacrifice the lives of others in the process? [Note: his plot also turned Joab into a co-conspirator in the deaths of all those men.] While David, certainly, did not want his adultery with Bathsheba to become public knowledge, it turns out his affair with Uriah's wife went far beyond the sin of adultery. He had something else to hide!

While scripture did say, "thou shalt not covet thy neighbor's wife" (Ex 20:17), there are different ways to violate the law. Adultery is wrong. However, the problem is compounded when a man commits adultery with the wife of his cousin or his brother or his friend or a national hero, etc. Things like that lead people to view the offense differently, and David knew he had stepped over the line.

Uriah the **What**?

In 2 Samuel 11 and 12, Uriah is named 22 times. There we read of David's adulterous affair, David ordering the death of Uriah, and the LORD sending Nathan to rebuke David. Apart from those passages there are only three other Old Testament references to Uriah.

We looked at one of them earlier, 1 Kings 15:5 where David's actions in this matter are referred to in terms of David turning aside from the commandment of the LORD "in the matter of Uriah the Hittite."

The other two verses where "Uriah the Hittite" was named turn out to be critical to a fuller understanding of the depth David had sunk to in this affair. Those verses are 2 Samuel 23:39 and 1 Chronicles 11:41. Taken out of context those verses tell us little, since they merely have his name documented and included in a list of other names. On the other hand, his name takes on great significance when those verses are read in context, because they are found in passages which tell us about David's "mighty men" (cf. 2 Sa 23:8-39, 1 Chr 11:11-47). Both passages have some men being described as "more honorable," but merely to be included in the list would have set those men apart from all of the other men in Israel.

Out of the thousands who served in the armies of Israel and out of all the men who lived in Israel in those days, very few ended up having their names noted in scripture with such a praiseworthy designation. Of all the names in the list of David's "mighty men," one of them truly jumps off the page – "Uriah the Hittite" (2 Sa 23:39, 1 Chr 11:41).

Uriah the "mighty" is not an idea that is often taught. Nevertheless, it is biblical. The reputation of Uriah is further confirmed when the term "the valiant men of the armies" (1 Chr 11:26) is applied to a group of men that explicitly includes "Uriah the Hittite" (1 Chr 11:41).

Half the Facts Versus Have the Facts

If we fail to consider the whole counsel of God and base our thinking on David's affair with Bathsheba and his murder of Uriah *only* on what we see in 2 Samuel 11 and 12, then our judgment of this episode will be based on incomplete data. This is because Uriah was not merely a soldier in the army; he was more like a war hero. Just as recipients of the Medal of Honor are highly esteemed by members of the U.S. military, the "mighty men" and "the valiant men of the armies" were probably held in high esteem by their fellow soldiers in Israel.

If we let scripture be a light to our path, then David's actions take on a wholly different quality. In our day, it would be akin to the difference between the Commander in Chief having an affair with the wife of a private in the army versus him sleeping with the wife of a war hero. David did not betray just anybody; he betrayed a man of renown.

Knowing who Uriah was starts to explain a lot of things. The palace was surely in the good part of town and Uriah lived within eyeshot of the king's palace with a relatively unobstructed view (cf. 2 Sa 11:2). One might expect to find a hero being rewarded for his efforts and this could be why Uriah ended up living so close to the king's palace.

The history of Uriah also reveals something else which casts a very dark cloud on the actions of David. David knew Uriah! Only a handful of men made the list of mighty men. So, David did not merely know of Uriah in the way one could be said to know a passing acquaintance. In addition, Uriah and Bathsheba lived in David's neighborhood.

Since Uriah was one of the "mighty men," David may have feared for his life after he got Bathsheba pregnant. Also, if the army learned one of the "mighty men" had been stabbed-in-the-back by David, it would create a far more problematic situation than would have been posed by the pregnancy of a stranger's wife. David had one heck of a motive to get rid of this threat to his reputation, his reign, and/or his life.

Uriah: A Man of Character

Uriah was one of "the valiant men of the armies" (cf. 1 Chr 11:26 & 41), so this may explain his affinity for his fellow troops and his willingness to deny himself pleasures that were denied to them because they were in an ongoing battle. [Another possibility is his act of self-denial could have been out of respect for the words "thou shalt love thy neighbor as thyself" (Lv 19:18).] As David found out, even getting Uriah drunk was not enough to compromise Uriah's loyalty to his fellow warriors.

Uriah's place among the "mighty men" casts David's affair with Bathsheba in a different light, and there is a question that is raised by the details found in scripture. If David knew Uriah before he slept with Uriah's wife, then was he also aware of her prior to the night of their adulterous get together? Is there reason to think he had been lusting after Uriah's wife **before** he decided to take her on the fateful night?

"And it came to pass in an evening, that David arose from off his bed, and walked upon the roof of the king's house: and from the roof he saw a woman washing herself; and the woman *was* very beautiful to look upon" (2 Sa 11:2). Reading those words in isolation could give one the impression of David accidentally spying Uriah's wife and being so smitten with her beauty that it drove him to behave badly in a spur of the moment decision. But is this conclusion justified by the evidence? Not if one considers all the facts.

<u>Why Did David Stay Behind?</u>

David was a man of war. Yet, in telling us about David's affair with Uriah's wife scripture says, "at the time when kings go forth *to battle*," he did not do so. Instead, "David tarried still at Jerusalem" (2 Sa 11:1).

The subsequent verses go on to tell us how he became involved with Uriah's wife, and how her pregnancy ultimately led him to kill one of his own "mighty men." The question remains, why did he stay behind? It was "the time when kings go forth *to battle*," but David "tarried still at Jerusalem." Why did he choose to act un-kingly and send his men off to war while he stayed home?

What if David knew Uriah's wife? Then he also knew staying behind while Uriah and his fellow soldiers were away would provide a window of opportunity in which Bathsheba would be separated from Uriah for an extended period of time. This verse records the time when David decided he would make his move: "David sent and enquired after the woman. And *one* said, *Is* not this Bathsheba, the daughter of Eliam, the wife of Uriah the Hittite?" (2 Sa 11:3).

Was David asking about a female whom he innocently laid eyes on as she happened to be "washing herself?" Notice the response to his inquiry: "And *one* said, *Is* not this Bathsheba, the daughter of Eliam, the wife of Uriah the Hittite?" While this may seem to be a mere report of information, those words may actually have been a warning and/or a rebuke to David, given the people who are mentioned. Ask yourself, why was her marriage cited last? Was this detail less important than who her father was?

Who was Bathsheba?

Why was Eliam (Bathsheba's father) mentioned first? Was it because he was a man of renown, who would also have been known to David? Like Uriah, Eliam was one of David's "mighty men." 2 Samuel 23:8 begins this way, "These *be* the names of the mighty men whom David had," and in the middle of the list it says, "Eliam the son of Ahithophel the Gilonite" (2 Sa 23:34).

So David messed with the wife of one of his "mighty men" and defiled the daughter of another of his "mighty men" in the same act. But wait, there is even more. Eliam was "the son of Ahithophel." Ahithophel is mentioned 20 times in the KJV. Note two things about him:

(A) he was "Ahithophel the Gilonite, David's counsellor" (2 Sa 15:12), and

(B) "the counsel of Ahithophel, which he counselled in those days, *was* as if a man had enquired at the oracle of God: so *was* all the counsel of Ahithophel both with David and with Absalom" (2 Sa 16:23).

So, what does this tell us?

It tells us the object of David's lust was not only the wife of one of his "mighty men." Bathsheba was also the daughter of another of those "mighty men" and she was the granddaughter of "David's counsellor." Therefore, given all of those close relationships to David, the chances of the beautiful Bathsheba being unknown to David are slim indeed!

Bathsheba lived in David's neighborhood and she also moved in the same circles. This is why David's problem of a pregnant Bathsheba was exponentially more complex. He did not kill Uriah simply because he wanted to avoid a public relations problem or a soiled reputation from being labeled an adulterer. The woman David defiled had ties to three men who were all close to him, notable, and/or very influential.

Moreover, even if someone still wants to assume David did not know Uriah's wife and had never laid eyes on her until he saw her "washing herself," there is still a problem. David was told:

(A) she was married,

(B) who she was married to, and

(C) who her father was (which would also have established who her grandfather was).

In spite of the personal ties he had to those men, David would not be denied his moment of pleasure. What in the world had happened to the one who was called, "a man after mine own heart" by God?

A Message from the LORD

As 2 Samuel 11 is about to end, it looks like David's cover up worked. Then the very last sentence says, "But the thing that David had done displeased the LORD" (2 Sa 11:27), and the opening of the next chapter tells of a message the LORD sent to David:

> "And the LORD sent Nathan unto David. And he came unto him, and said unto him, There were two men in one city; the one rich, and the other poor. The rich *man* had exceeding many flocks and herds: But the poor *man* had nothing, save one little ewe lamb, which he had bought and nourished up: and it grew up together with him, and with his children; it did eat of his own meat, and drank of his own cup, and lay in his bosom, and was unto him as a daughter. And there came a traveler unto the rich man, and he spared to take of his own flock and of his own herd, to dress for the wayfaring man that was come unto him; but took the poor man's lamb, and dressed it for the man that was come to him. And David's anger was greatly kindled against the man; and he said to Nathan, *As* the LORD liveth, the man that hath done this *thing* shall surely die: And he shall restore the lamb fourfold, because he did this thing, and because he had no pity" (2 Sa 12:1-6).

David apparently knew scripture so well that, without even thinking about it, he could immediately recall the "fourfold" prescription of the following penalty: "If a man shall steal an ox, or a sheep, and kill it, or sell it; he shall restore five oxen for an ox, and four sheep for a sheep" (Ex 22:1). Still, as we learn from many of the confrontations between Jesus and the religious experts of his day, just because people know the words in scripture does not guarantee they understand or obey those words.

In Exodus it also says, "thou shalt not covet thy neighbor's wife" (Ex 20:17). So David adopted a pick and choose approach to God's word prior to his adultery (instead of being diligent and showing respect for "every word of God"). When he pronounced the "fourfold" judgment he was totally blind to his own hypocrisy. However, this would change when Nathan spoke the words of rebuke that have become one of the most notable lines in all of the Old Testament, "Thou *art* the man":

"And Nathan said to David, Thou *art* the man. Thus saith the LORD God of Israel, I anointed thee king over Israel, and I delivered thee out of the hand of Saul; And I gave thee thy master's house, and thy master's wives into thy bosom, and gave thee the house of Israel and of Judah; and if *that had been too little*, I would moreover have given unto thee such and such things. Wherefore hast thou despised the commandment of the LORD, to do evil in his sight? Thou hast killed Uriah the Hittite with the sword, and hast taken his wife *to be* thy wife, and hast slain him with the sword of the children of Ammon. Now therefore the sword shall never depart from thine house; because thou hast despised me, and hast taken the wife of Uriah the Hittite to be thy wife" (2 Sa 12:7-10).

In 2 Samuel 7-10 we see Nathan, on behalf of the LORD, giving David an in-your-face rebuke. So, what are we to make of the first six verses of the chapter?

<u>Get to the Point?</u>

Though "the LORD sent Nathan unto David," Nathan did not go in and wag his finger in the king's face, and declare him to be an adulterer. Given all the *'give it to me straight,' 'cut to the chase,' 'get to the point'* kind of talk men like to toss around, it is likely many people think that approach to the truth is better. Is it? Nathan did not do that. Instead, he spent time presenting a teaching parable first.

When the LORD takes the time to paint a word picture of "two men in one city" it is worth our consideration. So, take a break from this book. Open your Bible, reread Nathan's words, and jot down your thoughts about them. Then come back to this case study and see if scripture can provide additional illumination on this topic.

End of Part One of the Case of David's Turn

The Case of David's Turn (Part Two)

<u>Truth and Consequences</u>

Now we will look at something David wrote following his adultery with the wife of Uriah. Then we will consider the *timing* of David's turn, as this may have something to do with why that instance of adultery was uniquely grievous in the eyes of the LORD. After that, we will examine Nathan's parable to see what it can teach us today.

Nathan pronounced a judgment, "The sword shall never depart from thine house" (2 Sa 12:10), and it was fulfilled in David's life from then on. The situation eventually led to this passage: "The sacrifices of God *are* a broken spirit: a broken and a contrite heart, O God, thou wilt not despise" (Ps 51:17). Those words have been a comfort to many readers of the Bible. But to fully grasp the truth behind those words, we need to consider them in their context and we find the context in this verse: "A Psalm of David, when Nathan the prophet came unto him, after he had gone into Bathsheba" (Ps 51:1).

When we know what occurred before David wrote Psalm 51, we can better appreciate having words like these included in scripture:

"Behold, thou [God] desirest truth in the inward parts: and in the hidden *part* thou shalt make me to know wisdom. Purge me with hyssop, and I shall be clean: wash me, and I shall be whiter than snow. Make me to hear joy and gladness; *that* the bones *which* thou hast broken may rejoice. Hide thy face from my sins, and blot out all mine iniquities. Create in me a clean heart, O God; and renew a right spirit within me" (Ps 51:6-10).

Actions have consequences. Moses made a statement along that line which should give us pause even to this day, "be sure your sin will find you out" (Nm 32:23). In the case of David, this is exactly what happened.

The moment of truth came when David looked to God's standard, and it led him to express righteous indignation:

"*As* the LORD liveth, the man that hath done this *thing* shall surely die: And he shall restore the lamb fourfold, because he did this thing, and because he had no pity" (2 Sa 12:5-6).

Undoubtedly, David assumed Nathan had presented him with a case requiring the king's judgment, and this <u>is</u> what occurred. However, he had no idea he was pronouncing judgment on himself.

Fit for a King

David knew what scripture said. Scripture contains special counsel and obligations for kings, including the following passage:

> "And it shall be, when he sitteth upon the throne of his kingdom, that he shall write him a copy of this law in a book out of *that which is* before the priests the Levites: And it shall be with him, and he shall read therein all the days of his life: that he may learn to fear the LORD his God, to keep all the words of this law and these statutes, to do them: That his heart be not lifted up above his brethren, and that he turn not aside from the commandment, *to* the right hand or *to* the left" (Dt 17:18-20).

It says, "he shall **read therein all the days of his life**" and this should lead us to consider how those words are connected to the daily needs mentioned in other Bible passages such as:

- "He [Jesus] said to *them* all, If any *man* will come after me, let him deny himself, and take up his cross daily" (Lk 9:23);
- "Give us day by day our daily bread" (Lk 11:3).

Did David "write him a copy of this law in a book" and "read therein all the days of his life" as a king was supposed to do? Apparently not, otherwise it may have kept him from taking Uriah's wife. How come? Because he missed out on the benefits set forth in the passage:

> "That he may learn to fear the LORD his God, to keep all the words of this law and these statutes, to do them: That his heart be not lifted up above his brethren, and **that he turn not aside from the commandment**, *to* the right hand, or *to* the left" (Dt 17:19-20).

[We are told, "David did *that which was* right in the eyes of the LORD, and turned not aside from any *thing* that he commanded him all the days of his life, save only in the matter of Uriah the Hittite" (1 Kgs 15:5). So, the question arises, might David's "turn" have been avoided if he had written out a copy of God's law and read from it "all the days of his life" as scripture said? (Would doing so still benefit people today?)]

A Royal Mess

The "well of Bethlehem" passage was considered in the introduction and it showed how much David valued the lives of his men in the days before he ascended to the throne. Nevertheless, David needed to be especially vigilant <u>after</u> he began to reign. Why is this? Stewardship!

He did not become king by accident of birth or conquest of a nation. "Thus saith the LORD God of Israel, I anointed thee king over Israel" is the declaration found in 2 Samuel 12:7.

David had been given the position. So, he was obliged to do right by the LORD who had blessed him with that leadership opportunity. Yet, in his choice to commit adultery with Uriah's wife, he did the opposite.

"Wherefore hast thou despised the commandment of the LORD, to do evil in his sight?" (2 Sa 12:9) One can almost hear the disappointment in those words, then the LORD expressed an even more personal note of indictment: "Thou hast despised **me**" (2 Sa 12:10).

David's violation of the LORD's trust made things exponentially worse than if the same deeds had been done by another man; and why this is true is made clear in these words, "By this deed thou hast given great occasion to the enemies of the LORD to blaspheme" (2 Sa 12:14). David's behavior was a reflection on the LORD, because the LORD had entrusted him with the position.

In Matthew 8:9 the term "a man under authority" described a man in a position of authority, who knew his orders were obeyed <u>because of the authority of the one who had put him there</u>. David "despised the commandment of the LORD," even though "the LORD God of Israel" was the one who anointed him "king over Israel" and had given him "the house of Israel and of Judah" (cf. 2 Sa 12:7-10).

Since his adultery was with the wife of one of his own "mighty men," it would have made the whole affair even more heinous in the eyes of men. Therefore, his actions did all the more to discredit the LORD who had made him king.

David was surely surprised when he heard, "thou *art* the man," and the words "thus saith the LORD God of Israel" (2 Sa 12:7) that came next were even weightier. But focusing solely on those items leads some people to gloss over Nathan's parable, missing an important lesson.

Nathan's report led David to unwittingly pronounce a judgment on his own behavior. He did not see himself in the parable, so his judgement regarding Nathan's report was not tilted in his favor by his own pride or prejudice. When Nathan went on to rebuke him, David learned he had actually pronounced judgment against himself.

The parable was a wake-up call for David, and it turns out the parable might also offer us a wake-up call regarding our Bible study method.

More than Meets the Eye

Here is just the parable portion of Nathan's message:

> "And the LORD sent Nathan unto David. And he came unto him, and said unto him, There were two men in one city; the one rich, and the other poor. The rich *man* had exceeding many flocks and herds: But the poor *man* had nothing, save one little ewe lamb, which he had bought and nourished up: and it grew up together with him, and with his children; it did eat of his own meat, and drank of his own cup, and lay in his bosom, and was unto him as a daughter. And there came a traveler unto the rich man, and he spared to take of his own flock and of his own herd, to dress for the wayfaring man that was come unto him; but took the poor man's lamb, and dressed it for the man that was come to him" (2 Sa 12:1-4).

Does it help people see the truth in the parable if a teacher tells them, *'David was the rich man, Uriah was the poor man, and Bathsheba was the lamb,'* or might it lead them to miss something in God's word?

"Every word of God *is* pure: he *is* a shield unto them that put their trust in him" (Prv 30:5) and looking to "every word of God" in this case can help to keep us from missing truth that is hidden in plain sight.

In the parable "The rich *man* had exceeding many flocks and herds: But the poor *man* had nothing, save one little ewe lamb" and the rich man "took the poor man's lamb." Do those characters in the parable readily correspond to what actually occurred? Yes. David already had multiple wives, and he also had an unknown number of concubines. Moreover, as king, he probably could have had his pick of almost any unmarried woman in the nation. In spite of this, he took Uriah's wife.

So, one can see some correlation between the parable and reality on those points. But if we think identifying "the rich *man,*" "the poor *man,*" and "the poor man's lamb" means we understand Nathan's parable, then we will be turned away from seeking the whole truth.

If our method of assessing truth leads us to assume we have solved the parable of "two men in one city" by seeing the rich man as David, the poor man as Uriah, and the lamb as Bathsheba, then our method will blind us to something God's word intended for us to wrestle with.

Who is the "traveler?"

Begging the Question

If "**every** word of God" is worthy of attention, then we also need to take note of the parable's fourth character. The passage is begging the question, who is the "traveler?" If our method led us to overlook this fourth character, then we know something about our method has to change. However, some who ignored the "traveler" will choose to tell themselves their method of assessing biblical truth works just fine and will dismiss the fourth character in the parable as irrelevant so they can avoid having to deal with this evidence. But is he irrelevant?

Is it reasonable for a person who says they respect the authority of the Bible and every part of God's word matters, to then argue out of the other side of their mouth that something in scripture is irrelevant? No. Either everything in God's word matters or some things can be dismissed as irrelevant, but people cannot have it both ways.

Those who say the "traveler" is irrelevant assume they get to dictate when scripture matters. By that standard, nothing in scripture matters unless *they* say it does. But is that a reasonable measure to use when weighing the words of scripture if one is really seeking the truth? No, because the truth matters whether we like it or not. A love of the truth would never lead one to downplay or turn from the light of God's word.

Attention to Detail

Diligence is encouraged in scripture. Readers of this case have had a chance to ponder the "traveler" and some will say he is unimportant, while others will realize he is worthy of attention. Those who respond to the biblical evidence (by changing their approach to scripture when it comes to this passage) will learn a lesson that could affect how they perceive other parables in the Bible.

Giving heed to what men say <u>about</u> God's word is not the same as giving heed <u>to</u> God's word. The truth is, men who claim the "traveler" in the parable is unimportant, do scripture an injustice.

Several facts testify to the importance of the "traveler." For example, in Nathan's parable he is referred to three times. Does this suggest he was irrelevant? No, it does not.

He is called by three different terms: "a traveler," "the wayfaring man," and "the man that was come to him," but a common factor clearly links all those terms. What those terms have in common is they all refer to the one who "came" to the rich man in the parable of Nathan, and in a few moments, we will take a look at this link.

Beyond his being mentioned three times, there is something else about the "traveler" that should immediately arrest our attention. But before we get to this, if you think it is not wise to simply brush aside the "traveler," then go back and look at the parable. Note everything we are told about "the rich *man*," "the poor *man*," "the poor man's lamb," and the "traveler." Then try to cite biblical evidence to prove each one's identity. [Those who are tempted to skip this step will, if they do so, only cheat themselves out of an exercise that can help to acclimate them to a better Bible study method.]

Hidden in Plain Sight

On many issues people who read God's word will often discover the answer was there all along, hidden in plain sight. Much of the time what keeps us from seeing it is a tradition we have been taught or an assumption we have made which leads us to overlook a truth that is clearly proven by the evidence in scripture.

If we take scripture at face value, we would be forced to conclude the trouble between the "two men in one city" (i.e., "the one rich, and the other poor") started when, "there came a traveler unto the rich man" (2 Sa 12:4). This is no small matter.

Why did the coming of the "traveler" prompt "the rich man" to take "the poor man's lamb" and how would this information help us identify the figures in the parable? The way to identify the figures in a parable is to let scripture show us how to do so. The attributes that are tied to each character must be the measure of whom that figure represents. Letting the attributes in God's word define the terms allows scripture to lead us to the answer.

In the case of Nathan's parable, what do we see? Among the details included in the parable were the following points:

(A) "the rich *man* had exceeding many flocks and herds,"
(B) "the poor *man* had nothing, save one little ewe lamb," and
(C) the rich man "took the poor man's lamb."

Since the parable is followed by Nathan's rebuke of David for taking Uriah's wife to be his own wife, it is easy to see a correlation between those attributes in the parable and reality on those points. However, the LORD inspired Nathan to go beyond a report of those three items. So, we should resist the methods of those who simply say, *'David is the rich man, Uriah is the poor man, and the lamb is Bathsheba,'* for doing so teaches people to be blind to the parable's fourth character.

The LORD led Nathan to include details about a "traveler," therefore one should not take away from God's word by acting like those details are not there or do not matter.

<u>Letting God's Word Teach Us</u>

A dictionary lists various attributes to help define a word and, in much the same way, the attributes recorded in scripture define the words or figures that have those attributes. In this case, the "traveler" is also called a "wayfaring man." It would be good if we looked to see how those terms were used elsewhere in scripture. Yet before doing so, we should first make sure we have considered all of the other details in the immediate context that is being studied.

We are told "a traveler" came "unto the rich man." He did not "take of his own flock and of his own herd, to dress for the wayfaring man that was come unto him; but took the poor man's lamb, and dressed it for the man that was come to him." Why did "the rich man" take "the poor man's lamb?" It was "for the wayfaring man that was come unto him." Notice the "lamb" was taken by "the rich man" and it was served to "the wayfaring man."

We need to go where scripture leads. If "the poor *man*" was intended to portray Uriah and "the poor man's lamb" portrays Bathsheba, then what must we conclude? The one who "took the poor man's lamb" was "the rich man," so this would have to be David because David was the one who took Uriah's wife. But in the parable "the poor man's lamb" is taken for and served to "the wayfaring man." Thus, scripture confronts us with this question: Who got the "lamb?"

When Nathan delivered the LORD's message to David it included this rebuke: "thou hast despised me, and hast taken the wife of Uriah the Hittite to be thy wife" (2 Sa 12:10). David took Uriah's wife and it is clear he took her for himself. Since "the wayfaring man" (i.e., the "traveler") got the "lamb" in the parable and David got Uriah's wife in reality, the evidence proves the "traveler" in Nathan's parable was David himself.

Of course, not everyone overlooks the parable's fourth character. Some who notice the "traveler" say, *'Satan is the traveler,'* and others awkwardly try to deal with the "traveler" by saying, *'the traveler is sin.'* However, several things are true. First, nowhere in Nathan's parable do we find any mention of Satan, the devil, demons, evil angels, etc., nor did the God-inspired writer of scripture use any of those terms anywhere else in the passage.

Second, a concept (sin) did not get Uriah's wife pregnant, David did. Sin never happens apart from a person (i.e., sin does not do itself), and superficial efforts to explain away the "traveler" need to give way to a diligent effort to thoughtfully weigh all the biblical evidence so we can do justice to the text.

Again, the attributes in the passage tell us "the poor man's lamb" was taken **by** "the rich man". It was taken for and given to a second figure. If "the poor man's lamb" portrayed Uriah's wife, then there is no way to get around the facts. Uriah's wife was taken **by** David and she was taken for and given to David. Thus, "the rich man" and the "traveler" portrayed the same person, David, before and after he gave into lust.

An Assumption and an Opportunity

What seems to blind many to the possibility that the "traveler" is David is a false assumption; they assume a fourth figure in the parable has to be a fourth person in reality. This is a good lesson in the application of Jesus' words "with what measure ye mete, it shall be measured to you." For, if we assume each character in a parable must correspond to a different person, then we will be unable to see any truth which does not fit our assumption.

When one of our assumptions is not true it will have the same effect as any prejudice. It will lead us to weigh the data using a false balance and the conclusions we reach will not be justified by the evidence. While it may *seem* reasonable to assume each character in a parable corresponds to a different person, we are not being led by God's word if we force scripture to conform to our understanding.

If biblical evidence could prove God's word demanded a one-to-one correspondence between parable and reality, then we would have a biblical justification on this point and we would not need to make an assumption. On the other hand, if we found even one time in scripture where one or more figures in a parable represented different aspects of the same person, what would we know? We would know it could also occur in other parables!

If a one-to-one assumption kept us from seeing the truth in this case, it could also do so on other parables. Hence, the correction offered by a biblical understanding of Nathan's parable can be far-reaching. This does not prove we have misunderstood other parables because of a false one-to-one assumption, but the possibility is there. So, the most reasonable thing to do would be to revisit the other parables in scripture and take another look at them in light of the realization that each character does not have to correspond to a different person.

Picture It This Way

No doubt, some recognized the "traveler" was David the moment they became aware of the fourth character. Still, seeing the "traveler" as David is only part of the lesson. If we initially missed the truth, then we need to figure out why we missed it.

Seeing David as both "the rich man" and "the wayfaring man" may cause some to bristle, for it might seem to be unreasonable given what is said of the "traveler" in the parable. We are told "there came a traveler unto the rich man" and twice more it refers to him as the one who "was come" to the rich man. So, is it reasonable to speak of a man coming to himself? Scripture does, and here are two examples so you can see how this expression was used:

- "when he <u>came to himself</u>, he said, How many hired servants of my father's have bread enough and to spare, and I perish with hunger" (Lk 15:17);
- "when Peter was <u>come to himself</u>, he said, Now I know of a surety, that the Lord hath sent his angel, and hath delivered me out of the hand of Herod, and *from* all the expectation of the people of the Jews" (Acts 12:11).

The first verse is from the parable of the prodigal son and the second is from the record of Peter being delivered out of prison in the Book of Acts. In both cases, a man *coming to himself* is a word picture that portrays a man having a moment of internal dialogue. He was doing what we all do; he was talking to himself. So, to think a man could not "come to himself" is to judge based on an assumption which cannot stand up to biblical scrutiny.

[Note the Hebrew word used in 2 Samuel 12:4 to tell of the figure who "came," was also used to refer to the coming of feelings such as: "fear", "pride", "shame", and "desire" (cf. Prv 1:27, 11:2, 13:12).]

According to scripture a man <u>can</u> "come to himself." The question is, did David do this when he chose to commit adultery with Uriah's wife?

Consider something Jesus said about adultery: "But I say unto you, That whosoever looketh on a woman to lust after her hath committed adultery with her already in his heart" (Mt 5:28). Some say that means *'thinking about adultery is the same as doing it'*. But Jesus did not say thinking about doing wrong is the same as doing wrong! The word "already" lets us know he was explaining a sequence – **before** a man can look "on a woman to lust after her," something must occur first.

The man must have "committed adultery with her already in his heart" because thoughts come before the behaviors they produce. So, in his statement, Jesus applied this truth to instances of lust (i.e., the act of looking "to lust" comes second; adultery in the "heart" comes first).

James 1:14 says, "every man is tempted, when he is drawn away of his own lust, and enticed," so this tells us what happened in the case of David's pursuit of Uriah's wife. Moreover, James 4:1 offers some additional insight on the problem of lust: "From whence *come* wars and fightings among you? *Come they* not hence, *even* of your lusts that war in your members?" This is found in the New Testament, yet there is every reason to think the problems between the "two men" in Nathan's parable sprang from the same root cause.

Truly, David turned out of the way and traveled away from the LORD when he sold himself on the idea of sleeping with Uriah's wife. But when he talked himself into it, who was involved in the conversation? He had the conversation with himself, and convinced himself to do it.

The Ultimate Reality

David was called a man after God's own heart (cf. 1 Sa 13:14, Acts 13:22-23). In order for David to do what he did to Uriah and with Bathsheba, **he first had to turn away from God** and there are many verses that make this point. First, note the LORD's rebuke of David, "Thou hast despised me, and hast taken the wife of Uriah the Hittite to be thy wife" (2 Sa 12:10). The sequence of those words may tell us something. Would it be correct to say that before David made his move on Uriah's wife, he first had to choose to ignore the LORD's authority and despise the counsel of the LORD that is provided in scripture?

What Jesus said about one who looks "on a woman to lust after her" lets us know it only happens when the one doing the looking "hath committed adultery with her already in his heart." Scripture tells us David "saw a woman washing herself" who was "very beautiful to look upon," and this would seem to qualify as looking "on a woman to lust after her" (and he may have even done so before that fateful night).

David "committed adultery" with Bathsheba "in his heart" prior to their physical union. The words of Jesus indicate it took place *before* David looked on her "to lust after her." In order for David to commit adultery "in his heart," he had to turn away from the light of scripture and the commandment that said, "Thou shalt not commit adultery" (Ex 20:14). David was rightly portrayed as a "traveler" because he moved away from being a man after God's own heart. He had the same body, but there was a man of a different character residing therein.

The Other Giant

David is famous for defeating Goliath in a great moment of courage and faith. When he was king and turned away from the LORD, David became his own worst enemy. Though David did not see it when he decided to take the wife of one of his "mighty men," his decision to turn away from the LORD put him in opposition to the LORD. Ironically, a giant named Goliath was the one who was in opposition to the LORD when David challenged him so many years before.

"David did *that which was* right in the eyes of the LORD, and turned not aside from any *thing* that he commanded him all the days of his life, save only in the matter of Uriah the Hittite" (1 Kgs 15:5). Notice what this reveals about David's behavior "in the matter of Uriah the Hittite." The rebuke is **not** primarily against an act of lust. It was a rebuke of the time when David "turned" – because in his choice to turn "aside" from the commandment, he was turning his back on the LORD.

Stories and old movies would use the image of a person dressed in white whispering good advice in their own right ear while at the same time the person was also pictured as dressed in black and whispering contrary advice in their other ear. It portrays one individual weighing their choices from two different perspectives. Which side will win? Unfortunately, when it came to Uriah's wife, David elected to cater to the appetites of "the wayfaring man that was come unto him." To do so, however, he had to first disregard what he knew to be right.

"The fear of man bringeth a snare: but whoso putteth his trust in the LORD shall be safe" (Prv 29:25). Unlike David's actions when he was standing before Goliath, his actions after he got Uriah's wife pregnant were founded on a fear of man: worrying about getting caught, the cover-up, etc. If a fear of God had been motivating David's actions, then he would not have done what he did. Notice how the principle of "A little leaven leaveneth the whole lump" played out in David's life. When he went against part of God's law, the rest of God's word was made of no effect unto him because he was not under God's authority (and in this state even murder seemed reasonable to him). "Purge out therefore the old leaven" is the advice of 1 Corinthians 5:7, and David had to repent of his disregard for the authority of God.

A Lesson in Humility

The LORD's rebuke was a lesson in humility for David and it is also a lesson for us. What it can teach us about our failure to be diligent in holding fast to God's word as the standard of truth should humble us.

David had disrespected the authority of God, but if we intentionally disregard a truth of scripture, are we not doing likewise?

As with everything in God's word, the verses on David's adulterous affair with the wife of Uriah have much to teach us. The method used in this case study has shown how letting God's word be the sole measure of truth can illuminate truths in scripture. Still, there remains much we have not considered. The many Psalms of David, the things that happened in David's life after he was rebuked by Nathan (i.e., by the LORD), how a son of David and Bathsheba fits in the lineage of Jesus, and many other things linked to David's adultery are available for your further consideration. [Proverbs 6 was not available to David, but it has some strong words to say regarding "he that goeth into his neighbor's wife" (Prv 6:29). This and other passages of scripture can shed even more light on the time when David "turned" aside.]

If you were previously satisfied with the usual treatment of the figures in Nathan's parable, you now know your method of assessing truth needs work. Explanations of the parable which ignore the "traveler" lead people to miss the whole truth, so a change of method is in order if we want to better understand God's word. If this study did its job, then it has shown there is no substitute for letting God's word be a lamp to our feet and a light to our path as we move through scripture.

While the first part of this study covered details about David, Uriah, and Bathsheba, one does not need all of that information to recognize there is a problem with the usual way of teaching Nathan's parable. There is a fourth character in the parable, but many people overlook this character or assume he is irrelevant merely because they do not see how a fourth figure can fit into the parable. However, those who gloss over or ignore the "traveler," will not see how Nathan's parable can help us to rightly discern other Bible parables.

The Conclusion of the Case of David's Turn

The importance of the "traveler" was not lost on David. When Nathan said, "Thou *art* the man," David did not have to wonder which man in the parable Nathan meant because David had taken "the poor man's lamb" **for himself**. In the parable, the LORD provided David a portrait of his actions, and the LORD can use this same parable to teach us.

If we ignored the "traveler," then we need to figure out why we did so. Receiving biblical correction involves more than switching our view on a particular point. In order to stand corrected, we also have to correct our method of assessing truth and this needs to be stressed when we share this insight with others.

If we have ever heard or read a teaching on Nathan's parable, then those things have shaped how we see it. Part of what leads people to miss the truth is when sermons or books treat the opinions of men as a reliable source of truth (rather than teaching people to weigh the biblical evidence). We must distinguish between the opinions of men and the evidence. If we do not do so, then we will be misled because we have used a false balance and our conclusions will not be based on the authority of God's word, even though we will be deceived into mistakenly assuming they are.

The evidence-based method used herein lets scripture teach us how to view the opinions of men and gives us a way to test our own beliefs. The Bible says, "Trust in the LORD with all thine heart; and lean not unto thine own understanding" (Prv 3:5), and one way we can do that is to always put our ideas to the test. The data we should judge by is the evidence in the word of God, and we know it is reliable because "all scripture *is* given by inspiration of God" (2 Tm 3:16).

As was stated earlier, these case studies cannot cover all the truth in God's word on the subjects being examined. In this instance, there is other evidence that may shed even more light on the mind of David in the days prior to his decision to sleep with Uriah's wife. This is left for the reader to pursue. But, to help show that all the data in scripture is worthy of our attention, consider these words:

> "...Joab smote Rabbah, and destroyed it. And David took the crown of their king from off his head, and found it to weigh a talent of gold, and *there were* precious stones in it; and it was set upon David's head" (1 Chr 20:1-2).

David had been anointed king by God's prophet. So, why did he want the crown of a foreign king to be on his head? What does this indicate about his mindset at the time? Then, compare 1 Chronicles 20:1 and 2 Samuel 11:1 and notice those passages refer to the same period. This raises another question – Was David wearing a foreign crown when he decided to take the wife of one of his mighty men and, if so, what does God mean us to learn from that picture?

The end of the Case of David's Turn

Chapter 3 – The Case of "the Eleven"

An Error in Scripture?

If we come across something in scripture that raises a difficulty for us or looks like an error in scripture, what should we do? If we assume there are mistakes in scripture, then our confidence in God's word will be shaken. The issue involved in this case does seem to raise an irreconcilable problem, which may explain why it is routinely ignored.

This case will show:

(A) how the teachings of men can keep people from seeing the answers that are available in scripture, and
(B) how God's word can teach us the truth even when it seems like we are faced with an impossible question.

The following occurred on the night of Jesus' resurrection: "he [Jesus] appeared unto the eleven as they sat at meat, and upbraided them with their unbelief and hardness of heart, because they believed not them which had seen him after he was risen" (Mk 16:14, cf. Lk 24:33-36). So, who were "the eleven?"

Since Judas was already dead (Mt 27:5) many people naturally assume "the eleven" means "the twelve" minus Judas. However, we must also consider this verse: "But Thomas, one of the twelve, called Didymus, was not with them when Jesus came" (Fourth gospel 20:24).

Neither Thomas nor Judas were there when Jesus met "the eleven," and twelve minus two is ten, not eleven. Therefore, we need to ask, how did Jesus meet with "the eleven" on that night? (When this issue is pointed out to people, sadly, some rush to assume the number was simply an error in scripture. This is not so.)

Now is your opportunity to check your Bible on this issue. Write down your thoughts about the answer. Then go on to the case study and see if the evidence presented can show how questions that are raised by scripture are best answered by God's word itself.

###

The Case of "the Eleven"

"The Twelve Apostles"

Revelation 21 describes "the holy city, new Jerusalem," and verse 14 says, "the wall of the city had twelve foundations, and in them the names of the twelve apostles of the Lamb." Some people say one of those names will be Paul and their rationale goes something like this:

> *'Paul was the apostle to the Gentiles and he wrote much of the New Testament. Obviously, God chose him to replace Judas as the twelfth apostle. In Acts 1, the disciples did not wait on God. Instead, they cast lots to replace Judas and picked someone who was never heard from again. Jesus himself chose Paul. Therefore, Paul became the twelfth apostle.'*

If you hear an idea like this taught, two things should raise a red flag. First, notice scripture does not require that conclusion; it is merely an inference from scripture being proposed. Second, to hold this idea, one has to discount the actions of Peter and the other disciples.

Erroneous teachings usually have some truth mixed in. For instance, Paul <u>was</u> mightily used by God, but men are adding to scripture when they then go on to say, *'Paul was the twelfth apostle.'* Citing scripture to disprove this idea does not disparage Paul in any way, for the idea has no biblical justification in the first place (as will be shown).

Worse yet, the whole idea requires one to assume that the actions of Peter and the other disciples can be set aside simply because they used "lots" to identify Judas' replacement (Acts 1:26).

What Does Scripture Tell Us?

After Jesus ascended into heaven, scripture says, "Peter stood up in the midst of the disciples" (Acts 1:15) and he spoke about Judas who had betrayed Jesus. He concluded with these words,

> "it is written in the book of Psalms, Let his [Judas'] habitation be desolate, and let no man dwell therein: and his bishopric let another take. Wherefore of these men which have companied with us all the time that the Lord Jesus went in and out among us, Beginning from the baptism of John, unto that same day that he was taken up from us, must one be ordained to be a witness with us of his resurrection" (Acts 1:20-22).

Then it says:

"They appointed two, Joseph called Barsabas, who was surnamed Justus, and Matthias. And they prayed, and said, Thou, Lord, which knowest the hearts of all *men*, shew whether of these two thou hast chosen, That he may take part of this ministry and apostleship, from which Judas by transgression fell, that he might go to his own place. And they gave forth their lots; and the lot fell upon Matthias; and he was numbered with the eleven apostles" (Acts 1:23-26).

Do those verses lead you to believe the disciples acted on their own? They prayed and asked for the Lord's guidance. Are we to believe the Lord did not hear their prayer? Some still insist the disciples did wrong because they cast lots in the process. But maybe the disciples knew the scriptures better than we do and maybe they believed what is said in Proverbs 16:33, "The lot is cast into the lap; but the whole disposing thereof *is* of the LORD."

We also have verses like:

- "by lot was their inheritance, as the LORD commanded by the hand of Moses" (Jos 14:2), and
- "the children of Israel gave by lot unto the Levites these cities with their suburbs, as the LORD commanded by the hand of Moses" (Jos 21:8).

The LORD, at times, wanted the "lot" to be used and yet some still say the disciples acted outside of God's will when they did so in Acts 1:26. Did the disciples do wrong when they used the "lot" to find out who God had chosen to take Judas' place among "the twelve?"

When men say *'Matthias was an illegitimate pick because God would later choose Paul,'* it is an example of how the teachings of men can use truth to sell a falsehood. While Paul **was** chosen to be an apostle, this did not make him Judas' replacement, and scripture proves Paul could not possibly have fulfilled that role.

What was Jesus' purpose in choosing Paul? Jesus told Paul:

"I have appeared unto thee for this purpose, to make thee a minister and a witness both of these things which thou hast seen, and of those things in which I will appear unto thee" (Acts 26:16).

The "purpose" that was stated by Jesus included nothing about Paul replacing Judas or being made one of "the twelve." Paul was called to be a "witness" of the things which he had seen and would see, but did that make him the replacement for Judas? No.

In his prior existence as Saul of Tarsus, Paul had not met Jesus prior to their conversation on the road to Damascus (cf. 1 Tm 1:13). Paul could be a "witness" to his encounters with Jesus from that point on, yet he could not "witness" to things he never saw.

Paul used the word "vision" to describe the appearance of Jesus to him on the Damascus Road (Acts 26:19). Given this "vision" and others, like the one noted in Acts 18:9, "Then spake the Lord to Paul in the night by a vision", Paul could testify as to Jesus being alive. However, "the twelve" saw things Paul never saw, including appearances of the risen Jesus in a flesh and bone body on earth before he was taken up into heaven.

In one of those appearances, Jesus showed himself to his disciples and said, "Behold my hands and my feet that it is I myself: handle me, and see; for a spirit hath not flesh and bones, as ye see me have" (Lk 24:39). Peter told the disciples one of them had to "be ordained to be a witness with us of his [Jesus'] resurrection" (Acts 1:22). Paul could not be that "witness" because he did not see what they saw, and a person would have to see what the disciples saw to be a witness "with" them.

Disciples, Apostles, and "the Twelve"

People often confuse biblical terms. A frequent error is to assume terms are synonymous when God's word is using different words to make distinctions. If someone said they saw a vehicle hit a vehicle and push it into an intersection where it was broadsided by another vehicle, you would have one impression. You would certainly have a very different impression if the person told you a bus hit a motorcycle and pushed it into an intersection where it was hit by an 18-wheeler. Both reports are correct, but one is more accurate.

We use different terms to make distinctions, and so does God's word. For example, in scripture the terms, "the disciples," "the apostles," and "the twelve" identify distinct categories. There is some overlap because "the twelve" were all apostles, and every apostle was also a disciple. Yet, not every disciple was an apostle, and not every apostle was one of "the twelve." We need to keep this in mind. There were many disciples and far fewer apostles. But "the twelve" singled out a unique group of men, and Paul was never called one of "the twelve."

More than twelve disciples were with Jesus throughout his earthly ministry. Notice what Peter said when he indicated the replacement for Judas needed to be one of "these men which have companied with us all the time that the Lord Jesus went in and out among us, Beginning from the baptism of John, unto that same day that he was taken up from us" (Acts 1:21-22). At one point, Jesus chose twelve of his disciples and he named them "apostles" (Mt 10:1-2, Mk 3:13-14, Lk 6:13).

In the Bible, the terms "the twelve" and "apostles" denote the same subset of disciples until the term "apostle" came to be used of others, such as Barnabas, Paul, and James (Acts 14:14, Gal 1:19), etc. There are more than twelve apostles in scripture, but the number in "the twelve" was always twelve. When Judas forfeited his position in the group, he was replaced. Thereafter, "the twelve" referred to the same group, only with Matthias having taken the place ("the bishopric") of Judas.

Scripture says, "the lot fell upon Matthias; and he was numbered with the eleven apostles" (Acts 1:26). Just a few verses later we are told about "Peter, standing up with the eleven" on the day of Pentecost (Acts 2:14). Peter did not stand up with 'the ten', so this verse confirms Matthias was one of "the twelve" – because Matthias had to be one of "the twelve" or else Peter could not have stood up "with the eleven." Also, Acts 6:2 says, "the twelve called the multitude of the disciples," and the term "the twelve" in this verse can make no sense without Matthias (since Saul/Paul had not yet been introduced in scripture).

The Apostle Matthias

Acts 2:14 tells of "Peter, standing up with the eleven." The author of Acts later referred to this group of men as, "Peter" and "the rest of the apostles" (Acts 2:37). The term "apostles" was used this same way **more than a dozen times** before Saul of Tarsus is even mentioned (Acts 2:42, 43, 4:33, 35, 36, 37, 5:2, 12, 18, 29, 34, 40, 6:6), so the author of Acts clearly believed Matthias replaced Judas and was "numbered with the eleven apostles" (just as the author's words in Acts 1:26 show).

Men who say Paul was the twelfth apostle ignore the verses that show Matthias was included in "the twelve." They also ignore Peter's words:

"It is written in the book of Psalms, Let his [Judas'] habitation be desolate, and let no man dwell therein: and his bishopric let another take. Wherefore of these men which have companied with us all the time that the Lord Jesus went in and out among us, Beginning from the baptism of John, unto that same day that he was taken up from us, must one be ordained to be a witness with us of his resurrection" (Acts 1:20-22).

45

The one who would take Judas' "bishopric" was not merely filling an open slot among "the twelve." Peter told the disciples the man would be "ordained to be a witness with us of his [Jesus'] resurrection." This is why Peter said the man needed to be one of the "men which have companied with us all the time that the Lord Jesus went in and out among us, beginning from the baptism of John, unto that same day that he was taken up from us." Thus, those who say Paul was the twelfth apostle are ignoring the whole purpose for replacing Judas.

Those who believe Paul was the replacement for Judas create a problem for themselves which cannot be reconciled. When Jesus met with "the eleven" on the day of his resurrection, Thomas was the one of "the twelve" who was missing (cp. Mk 16:14, Lk 24:33, Fourth gospel 20:24). Therefore, Judas' replacement had to be present at that event, since only one of "the twelve" was missing.

Biblical Answers to Bible Questions

Admittedly, the identity of "the eleven" might not be readily apparent. Nevertheless, scripture provides all of the data we need to answer the question if we let God's word be the measure of truth. Consider what we are told about Matthias. He was a loyal follower of Jesus and was there with the disciples "all the time that the Lord Jesus went in and out among" them, "beginning from the baptism of John, unto that same day that he was taken up" into heaven. So, Matthias was there throughout Jesus' ministry (cf. Acts 1:21-22).

More important, Peter's words prove Matthias was with the disciples on the day Jesus was taken up into heaven. This must affect our view of what is said about that day in Acts 1:2-4:

"the day in which he [Jesus] was taken up, after that he through the Holy Ghost had given commandments unto the apostles whom he had chosen: To whom also he shewed himself alive after his passion by many infallible proofs, being seen of them forty days, and speaking of the things pertaining to the kingdom of God: And, being assembled together with *them*, commanded them that they should not depart from Jerusalem, but wait for the promise of the Father, which, *saith he*, ye have heard of me."

The writer of Acts included Matthias with the "apostles" in reporting the events on the day of Pentecost (cf. Acts 2:14 & 37) and used the term "apostles" in reporting Jesus was "taken up, after that he through the Holy Ghost had given commandments unto the apostles whom he had chosen."

A person may want to say the word "apostles" in Acts 1:2 only refers to the original twelve minus Judas. Still, we need to realize the writer of Acts already knew Matthias was the replacement for Judas at the time he wrote those words (i.e., verses 2-4).

Since Acts 1:2 referred to "the apostles whom he [Jesus] had chosen," someone may try to say this limits the term "apostles" in this verse to the remaining eleven original members of "the twelve." But the writer of Acts also told us what occurred after Jesus was taken up and the disciples returned unto Jerusalem (Acts 1:12). We are told they gathered together in an upper room and:

> "they prayed, and said, Thou, Lord, which knowest the hearts of all *men*, shew whether of these two thou hast chosen, That he may take part of this ministry and apostleship, from which Judas by transgression fell" (Acts 1:24-25).

Notice the past tense in their prayer request, "shew whether of these two thou **hast chosen**." This lets us know the disciples believed the Lord had already chosen a replacement for Judas.

In that prayer, they were not asking the Lord to make a choice. Rather, they were asking the Lord to show them who he had chosen. While "Jesus knew from the beginning who they were that believed not, and who should betray him" (Fourth gospel 6:64), the disciples only learned who the betrayer was after the fact. In Acts 1:15-26 the same sort of thing occurred; the betrayer's replacement had already been chosen, but the disciples learned who it was only after the lot identified him.

Learning What God Already Knows

Acts 15:18 says, "known unto God are all his works from the beginning of the world." So, those who were with Jesus throughout his ministry recognized this after he rose from the dead. Moreover, we are told, "Jesus knew from the beginning" who would betray him. No options. No possibilities. No way a different disciple could have been the one to betray him. Jesus knew who his betrayer was and events were not going to prove him wrong. More than once, Jesus had said he would be betrayed (Mt 17:22, 20:18, 26:2, et al.). In spite of this, the other disciples failed to recognize who the betrayer was until Judas brought men to arrest Jesus in the garden of Gethsemane and Jesus explicitly said Judas had betrayed him "with a kiss" (Lk 22:48). Also, Jesus died and rose from the dead just as he had said. Therefore, after he rose from the dead his disciples surely realized he knew things before they did.

The events in Acts 1 occurred before the gospels were written. Thus, the gospel writers knew the Lord had chosen Matthias to take the "ministry and apostleship, from which Judas by transgression fell" (Acts 1:25), and this is reflected in their words. When Mark 16:14 and Luke 24:33-36 tell of Jesus meeting with "the eleven" late on the day when he rose from the dead, the term "the eleven" included Matthias (as it does in Acts 2:14) and it excluded Thomas, who was not present (Fourth gospel 20:24). Judas was no longer in the group because his part in the "ministry and apostleship" was lost in his act of "transgression."

The phrase "one of the twelve" applied to Judas up until he arrived at the garden and betrayed Jesus with a kiss (Mt 26:47, Mk 14:43, Lk 22:47). From that point on, Judas was never again referred to as a disciple or "one of the twelve" and, of course, he was not included in Acts 1:13 when the remaining original apostles were listed.

The Conclusion to the Case of "the Eleven"

Men who refuse to believe Matthias replaced Judas create a problem for themselves on the issue of who was present when Jesus met with "the eleven" on that evening. On the other hand, if we let scripture be a lamp to our feet (show us where to stand on an issue) and a light to our path (show us where to go with a thought), then the whole counsel of God's word is able to teach us and help us grow.

Those who see Paul as the 'real' replacement for Judas will often say, 'Matthias is never mentioned again after Acts 1!' They emphasize this to make him look illegitimate, but their inference is shown to be false if it is subjected to biblical scrutiny. In Acts 1:12 "Andrew," "Thomas," and "Bartholomew" are named and, from then on, they are not named again in scripture. Were they insignificant or irrelevant? No, that is a false inference (whether it is used against Bartholomew or Matthias). Nevertheless, men sometimes draw false inferences from true facts. This is why it is important to put every idea to the test of scripture.

Some claim there is not sufficient evidence to prove the identification of Matthias by "lot" was valid, yet, this is not so. We know Matthias was chosen by God because scripture requires it, or else terms like "the eleven" make no sense. Similarly, the risen Jesus appeared to "the twelve" (1 Cor 15:5), and this proves the inspired writer of scripture counted Matthias among "the twelve" (because 1 Corinthians 15:3-8 gives a sequence of events that shows his reference to "the twelve" had to include Matthias). [Go read those verses to see this yourself.]

The end of the Case of the Eleven

Chapter 4 – The Case of John's Question

Reasonable Doubt?

John the Baptist is a famous New Testament figure. Scripture reports the miracle of his birth (Lk 1:5-25, 36-44 & 57-80). It also lets us know John was a relative of Jesus because scripture tells us John's mother was a cousin of the mother of Jesus (Lk 1:36). Jesus was baptized by John and "John bare record, saying, I saw the Spirit descending from heaven like a dove, and it abode upon him" (Fourth gospel 1:32).

Scripture tells us many things about John, including this fact; he had been put in prison by Herod, "for John had said unto Herod, It is not lawful for thee to have thy brother's wife" (Mk 6:18). Scripture also says while John was in prison he sent two of his disciples to ask Jesus, "Art thou he that should come, or do we look for another?" (Mt 11:2-3, Lk 7:19). So, what are we to make of John's question?

This is the time to get your Bible and look at John's question. Jot down your thoughts about it, then return to this case study to compare your notes to the evidence that will be presented to see if scripture reveals a better way to gain insight on John's curious question.

###

The Case of John's Question

John the Baptist Asked Jesus a Question

"Art thou he that should come, or do we look for another?" (Mt 11:3, Lk 7:19). Given the other things John the Baptist said about Jesus, many wonder why he would ask this of Jesus. In an effort to make sense of the question, people ascribe various motives to John, and this usually leads them to characterize his inquiry in one of the following ways:

(A) *'John had a moment of doubt, but since he was in prison at the time he would have been depressed, so his doubt about Jesus is understandable;'*
(B) *'John was discouraged so he wondered if Jesus was truly the Christ;'*
(C) *'John was perplexed and/or frustrated because Jesus had not yet overthrown the Romans as John had expected;'* or
(D) *'John knew who Jesus was and he only asked the question because he wanted his disciples to know it too.'*

Sadly, ideas like those pass for sound reasoning with alarming ease, due to our tendency to lean on our own understanding, and our desire to get a fast answer without having to search the scriptures. However, as will be shown, those views cannot stand up to biblical scrutiny.

Doubting John?

The Bible says, "Every word of God *is* pure: he *is* a shield unto them that put their trust in him" (Prv 30:5), and it surely applies in this case. Notice John's question does not mention "the Christ." Still, people will rush to judgment and assume that is what he was asking about (and this leads them to hold views like the ones listed above). Do they cite scripture to show "the Christ" was the subject of John's question? No. They take it for granted, and because they can find others who agree with them, they assume they are correct. But, agreement among men is no assurance of truth.

In scripture John did not call Jesus "the Christ," but when he baptized Jesus he "saw the Spirit descending from heaven like a dove, and it abode upon" Jesus (Fourth gospel 1:32). John also declared Jesus to be "the Lamb of God" (Fourth gospel 1:29 & 36). When John's disciple Andrew heard this, he left to follow Jesus and *the next day* he told his brother Peter, "We have found the Messiah, which is, being interpreted, the Christ" (Fourth gospel 1:41). So, Andrew knew Jesus was "the Christ" and this suggests Andrew learned this from his mentor John the Baptist.

Because of all that, those who presume John's question was about "the Christ" have to find ways to explain his question. For example, John was in prison when he asked it, so some say, 'he was depressed and he just had a moment of doubt like we all do.' But would being in prison always lead a man of God to be depressed? No. In Acts 16:23 Paul and Silas were cast "into prison" and they "prayed, and sang praises unto God" (Acts 16:25). While this does not prove John was not depressed when he sent his question to Jesus, it shows it is wrong to assume he was depressed just because he was in prison at the time. Moreover, his execution came as a surprise (Mt 14:6-10, Mk 6:20-27), so those who say he depressed because of that are ignoring the facts.

Besides identifying Jesus as "the Lamb of God" and seeing "the Spirit descending from heaven like a dove" and abiding on Jesus, John was "filled with the Holy Ghost, even from his mother's womb" (Lk 1:15). John's mother would surely have told him about his own miracle birth along with whatever details she learned from her cousin Mary about the birth of Jesus. In order to believe John was asking if Jesus was "the Christ," we must assume John forgot or ignored all this evidence. He also said, "one mightier than I cometh, the latchet of whose shoes I am not worthy to unloose" (Lu 3:16). Did he later do an about-face and think he *was* worthy to question if Jesus *was* "the Christ?" If not, then we must reject that idea, realize his question had a different purpose, and allow scripture to teach us how to see it from John's point of view.

The Context of the Question

Instead of considering John's question in isolation and out of context, we need to see what moved John to ask the question. In Matthew 11, John's question is found in this context:

"it came to pass, when Jesus had made an end of commanding his twelve disciples, he departed thence to teach and to preach in their cities. Now when John had heard in the prison the works of Christ, he sent two of his disciples, And said unto him, Art thou he that should come, or do we look for another?" (Mt 11:1-3).

Notice it does not say John heard about the works of 'Jesus.' It says he heard "the works of Christ." Is there any biblical reason to believe such a report would either frustrate John, or prompt him to wonder if Jesus was "the Christ?" No.

If John already knew Jesus was "the Christ," then why did this report of "the works of Christ" cause John to ask the question that he did?

Thankfully, scripture has another account of John's question. In this passage, we find additional details about the report that moved John to send a question to Jesus. Furthermore, this additional information also helps us to see why John phrased his question in the way he did.

Luke 7:11-19 presents the following report:

"And it came to pass the day after, that he [Jesus] went into a city called Nain; and many of his disciples went with him, and much people. Now when he came nigh to the gate of the city, behold, there was a dead man carried out, the only son of his mother, and she was a widow: and much people of the city was with her. And when the Lord saw her, he had compassion on her, and said unto her, Weep not. And he came and touched the bier [platform to carry a body]: and they that bare *him* stood still. And he said, Young man, I say unto thee, Arise. And he that was dead sat up, and began to speak. And he delivered him to his mother. And there came a fear on all: and they glorified God, saying, That a great prophet is risen up among us; and, That God hath visited his people. And this rumor of him went forth throughout all Judea, and throughout all the region round about. And the disciples of John shewed him of all these things. And John calling *unto him* two of his disciples sent *them* to Jesus, saying, Art thou he that should come or look we for another?"

John Gets Some Good News!

"And the disciples of John shewed him of all these things" (Lk 7:18). What did he learn from their report? He learned about Jesus raising a man from the dead and the reaction that followed. Would this cause John to doubt or be impatient? No. (Also, John's disciples brought him the news. So, those who say he asked the question 'for their benefit' need to realize they knew of "the works of Christ" before John did.)

Of course, one might doubt a report of Jesus raising someone from the dead. However, if a person knew it was true, it would not cause them to doubt Jesus. For example, when the religious leaders heard about Jesus raising Lazarus from the dead, they did not doubt Jesus; they plotted to kill him (cf. Fourth gospel 11:43-53).

John's disciples told him about the miracle and the crowd's reaction. Because he trusted their report and learned new information, he sent a question to Jesus. We can learn this if we look to scripture to see what led him to ask it. But if his question is considered by itself, then we can easily misunderstand his words because they are cut off from the rest of scripture.

Jesus on John the Baptist

Jesus' words also let us know John's question did not indicate doubt on John's part, for <u>after</u> he heard John's question he said, "Among those that are born of women there is not a greater prophet than John the Baptist" (Lk 7:28). Jesus said those words after John's disciples left to bring him Jesus' response. Here is his statement in context:

"And when the messengers of John were departed, he [Jesus] began to speak unto the people concerning John, What went ye out into the wilderness for to see? A reed shaken with the wind? But what went ye out for to see? A man clothed in soft raiment? Behold, they which are gorgeously appareled, and live delicately, are in kings' courts. But what went ye out for to see? A prophet? Yea, I say unto you, and much more than a prophet. This is *he*, of whom it is written, Behold, I send my messenger before thy face, which shall prepare thy way before thee. For I say unto you, Among those that are born of women there is not a greater prophet than John the Baptist: but he that is least in the kingdom of God is greater than he. And all the people that heard *him*, and the publicans, justified God, being baptized with the baptism of John" (Lk 7:24-29).

Do those words suggest John's question indicated doubt, impatience, depression, wavering, or a weak moment on his part? No they do not. Jesus' criticized his own disciples in their moments "of little faith" (Mt 6:30, 8:26, 14:31, 16:8), but he said no such words about John.

On the contrary, after Jesus responded to John's question, he said, "Among those that are born of women there is not a greater prophet than John the Baptist." Those words do not suggest he thought John was doubting or frustrated or perplexed.

Some may still try to defend the *'doubting John'* idea by suggesting it is justified because Jesus also said this to the two disciples of John, "And blessed is *he*, whosoever shall not be offended in me" (Mt 11:6, Lk 7:23). Those words were <u>part</u> of Jesus' response to John's question, and it is fair to ask, what did Jesus mean by those words? Yet, to assume the phrase "offended in me" justifies the *'doubting John'* idea one has to ignore:

(A) what led John to ask the question, and
(B) the words of praise about John that were spoken by Jesus right after he sent his response to John.

Cause and Effect

People do not usually ask a question when they think they already know the answer. If someone says, *'John asked Jesus if he was really the Messiah'* and we believe them, then that will define how we see John's question. When we discover there is evidence to the contrary, then we will begin to wonder, what was John asking? As you will see, the key to discovering the intent of John's question is to let scripture teach us why he asked it.

Luke 7:11-14 tells us Jesus visited "a city called Nain" where "a dead man was carried out" who was "the only son of his mother, and she was a widow" and Jesus "had compassion on her" and raised her son from the dead right then and there. Here is what happened after that:

> "...he that was dead sat up, and began to speak. And he [Jesus] delivered him to his mother. And there came a fear on all: and they glorified God, saying, That a great prophet is risen up among us; and, That God hath visited his people. And this rumor of him went forth throughout all Judea, and throughout all the region round about. And the disciples of John shewed him of all these things. And John calling *unto him* two of his disciples sent *them* to Jesus, saying, Art thou he that should come, or look we for another?" (Lk 7:15-19).

In paying attention to "every word of God" always note the sequence in which scripture presents the facts. John's question came after he heard of "all these things." This means the miracle Jesus did was not the only thing John heard about. "All these things" would also have included the crowd's response to the miracle.

"And they glorified God"

"There came a fear on all: and they glorified God, saying, That a great prophet is risen up among us; and, That God hath visited his people" (Lk 7:16). No doubt a flood of emotions swept over the people who saw Jesus do the miracle. Given how fans today react at a ball game, one may be tempted to think of this as a time when the crowd went wild. Scripture paints a very different picture, however.

It says, "there came a fear on all." This is far different than euphoria. It is more like how the disciples reacted when Jesus stopped a storm (Mt 8:26, Mk 4:39, Lk 8:24). They were afraid of the storm, but when Jesus stopped the storm, they "marveled" (Mt 8:27), and "feared exceedingly" (Mk 4:41), and asked one another "What manner of man is this?" while "they being afraid wondered" (Lk 8:25).

"And there came a fear on all" describes a profound awe. This lets us know the words "and they glorified God" do not suggest the crowd cheered or jumped for joy. Rather, those eyewitnesses recognized the miracle of Jesus raising the widow's son from the dead was far more than just a great gift. They had seen God's hand at work and their response was to glorify God. John heard about both the miracle and the response of the eyewitnesses in the aftermath of the miracle – and this is what led John the Baptist to ask Jesus a question.

Scripture versus Our Assumptions

The idea that John's question had to do with Jesus being "the Christ" does not arise from scripture. That assumption needs to be subjected to biblical scrutiny. Once it is, then the facts in the word of God can open our eyes to true intent of John's question.

When we read the Bible, we tend to view things through the lens of our present beliefs (i.e., we lean on our own understanding). Since we assume our beliefs are correct, we think the men of God whom we read about in scripture would think like us. However, we know things the people of John's day did not know, so we need to avoid imposing our views on the text. The way to do this is to let scripture teach us the views of the people we are reading about.

Churchgoers are taught to see Jesus as prophet, priest, and king, but the people who lived in John's day had a different perspective than post-resurrection believers do. No doubt John had more insight about Jesus than others did in that era. Nevertheless, he had a first century, pre-resurrection perspective. Therefore, to understand his question, we must see it from his point of view.

John Asked the Right Question

Why would the miracle, and the crowd's reaction to it, inspire John to ask Jesus, "Art thou he that should come, or look we for another?" John did not ask, 'Was I wrong?' or 'Are you really the Lamb of God?' (Then he would have been doubting.) Instead, he asked if Jesus was "he **that should come**." When people make a rush to judgment and assume this term referred to the Christ, they are leaning on their own understanding, and they misconstrue his question. As will be shown, John's knowledge of Jesus was actually growing when he asked it.

There was an air of anticipation in that era, as we see in Luke 3:15 – "**The people were in expectation**, and all men mused in their hearts of John, whether he were the Christ, or not." Yet, to understand how people in that day viewed Jesus, we need to recognize "the Christ" was not the only person they were expecting!

After the miracle people said, "a great prophet is risen up among us," and hearing of those things caused John to ask if Jesus was "he **that should come.**" Why? Scripture has the answer, for it proves the Jews of John's day were waiting for someone other than "the Christ."

They were also looking for...

The Prophet That Should Come

Moses said, "The LORD thy God will raise up unto thee a Prophet from the midst of thee, of thy brethren, like unto me" (Dt 18:15). Moses spoke of a prophet to come and this was highlighted again when the LORD told Moses, "I will raise them up a Prophet from among their brethren, like unto thee, and will put my words in his mouth; and he shall speak unto them all that I shall command him" (Dt 18:18). It was Moses who communicated this prophecy, and it was stated this prophet would be "like unto" Moses. The Jews who esteemed Moses would have looked forward to the fulfillment of this prophecy, and given his prominence in Israel's history, this promise would have been high on their list of expectations. In John's day, terms such as "that prophet" and the one "that should come" were used to refer to this person, as will be shown.

[The Old Testament prophets had come and gone and none of them were the fulfillment of this prophecy. This is also true of Elijah, though scripture has a separate prophecy related to him: "Behold, I will send you Elijah the prophet before the coming of the great and dreadful day of the LORD" (Mal 4:5).]

In John's time, there was an unfulfilled prophecy delivered *by* Moses, about one who would be "like unto" Moses. So, it should not surprise anyone to learn the Jews were looking for this prophecy to be fulfilled. However, it may come as a surprise to many churchgoers today when they learn the people of John's day thought the prophecies regarding "that prophet" and "the Christ" spoke of two people, not one person.

Getting to Know Jesus

People cannot make sense of John's question until they see that, at the time of Jesus' ministry, God's faithful did not view Jesus the way we do now. This included John the Baptist who, like those of his day, believed the prophet to come was a separate person from the Christ – or at least he did until he was moved to pose his question to Jesus.

"All men mused in their hearts of John, whether he were the Christ, or not" (Lk 3:15). They also had other ideas as to who John might be, as we can see from this passage:

"And this is the record of John, when the Jews sent priests and Levites from Jerusalem to ask him, Who art thou? And he confessed, and denied not; but confessed, I am not the Christ. And they asked him, What then? Art thou Elias? And he saith, I am not. Art thou that prophet? And he answered, No" (Fourth gospel 1:19-21).

Note the three options: "the Christ," "Elias," or "that prophet." This is where we learn those designations were seen as distinct individuals in that era. The "priests and Levites" who asked John those questions clearly thought "that prophet" and "the Christ" were different people. Others "which were sent were of the Pharisees" (Fourth gospel 1:24), also asked John about the same options: "Why baptizest thou then, if thou be not that Christ, nor Elias, neither that prophet?" (Fourth gospel 1:25). He did not correct those who asked him those questions. At that time, John did not say anything that would suggest he thought "the Christ" and "that prophet" would be one individual. Keep this in mind.

People living in John's day assumed the role of "that prophet" would be fulfilled by one person and someone else would fulfill the role of "the Christ." While John was a prophet and a cousin of Jesus (Lk 1:36), his knowledge of Jesus was not complete, for John himself twice said, "I knew him not" (Fourth gospel 1:31 & 33). Thus, we should not be shocked to find John discovering a new insight about Jesus.

The guesswork regarding John pales by comparison to the debates about Jesus. For the most part, John was well thought of in his day, "all *men* counted John, that he was a prophet indeed" (Mk 11:32), but Jesus polarized the people. Although Jesus was working miracles that nobody else had done, public opinion about him was often split and contentious, as Jesus said it would be.

<u>Division Caused by Jesus</u>

"Suppose ye that I am come to give peace on earth? I tell you, Nay; but rather division" (Lk 12:51). Jesus spoke those words and he did as he said. We are told "there was a division among the people because of him" (Fourth gospel 7:43). Similar language was used to describe the opposing reactions to Jesus on two other occasions: "And there was a division among them" (Fourth gospel 9:16) and "There was a division therefore again among the Jews" (Fourth gospel 10:19).

We see a wide range of opinions regarding Jesus. When Jesus asked his disciples, "Whom say the people that I am?" (Lk 9:18) they replied, "John the Baptist; but some *say*, Elias; and others *say*, that one of the old prophets is risen again" (Lk 9:19). A parallel account in Matthew 16:14 has "and others, Jeremiah" also thrown into this mix. [Note: the speculation about Jesus being "John the Baptist" occurred after John had been beheaded, and it lets us know some people thought Jesus was John risen from the dead (cf. Lk 9:7-8).] What should arrest our attention is not the various ideas as to who Jesus was, rather, it is what is missing from the list. Notice "the Christ" is not even included in that list!

In the verses above we saw when the "priests and Levites" and "they which were sent were of the Pharisees" quizzed John the Baptist, "the Christ" was at the top of their list of speculations about who John was. This was not the case when it came to Jesus. Still, it is possible Jesus may have wanted it that way, for when he went on to ask his disciples, "But whom say ye that I am?" and Peter said, "the Christ," Jesus then told his disciples to "tell no man" (cf. Mt 16:15-16 & 20, Mk 8:29-30, Lk 9:20-21). So, Jesus was obviously not seeking to publicize his role as Christ at that point in time.

While Jesus did not proclaim he was "the Christ," some still knew it. Andrew was the first disciple in scripture to publicly declare it when "he first findeth his own brother Simon, and saith unto him, We have found the Messiah, which is, being interpreted, the Christ" (Fourth gospel 1:41). The woman at the well also figured out who Jesus was. Her first assessment of him was, "Sir, I perceive that thou art a prophet" (Fourth gospel 4:19). Then after learning more, she left Jesus and told the men of her city, "Come, see a man, which told me all things that ever I did: is not this the Christ?" (Fourth gospel 4:29). After the men of the city spent two days with Jesus, then they agreed with her conclusion and said, "we have heard *him* ourselves, and know that this is indeed the Christ" (Fourth gospel 4:42). "The twelve" came to know it (cf. Fourth gospel 6:69). Martha also called Jesus "the Christ" <u>before</u> he raised her brother Lazarus (Fourth gospel 11:27).

Once when Jesus was in the temple some said, "He speaketh boldly, and they say nothing unto him. Do the rulers know indeed that this is the very Christ? ... And many of the people believed on him, and said, When Christ cometh, will he do more miracles than these which this *man* hath done?" (Fourth gospel 7:26 & 31). Jesus' works plainly testified as to who he was – so much so that when the Jews said, "How long will thou make us to doubt? If thou be the Christ, tell us plainly. Jesus answered them, I told you, and ye believed not" (Fourth gospel 10:24-25).

Despite the miracles he did, the debates over Jesus did not cease. His opponents tried to sow doubts about him among the people, and this fueled the debate, as in this verse: when some of the Pharisees said, "This man is not of God, because he keepeth not the sabbath day. Others said, How can a man that is a sinner do such miracles? And there was a division among them" (Fourth gospel 9:16).

Another time "many of them [the Jews] said, He hath a devil, and is mad; why hear ye him? Others said, These are not the words of him that hath a devil. Can a devil open the eyes of the blind?" (Fourth gospel 10:20-21).

At a different time we read, "there was much murmuring among the people concerning him: for some said, He is a good man: others said, Nay; but he deceiveth the people" (Fourth gospel 7:12).

"That prophet that should come into the world"

When Jesus came onto the scene, the people were looking for the Christ, Elijah, and the prophet like unto Moses – and two passages record occasions when some people saw Jesus as a possible candidate for the latter of those three.

The first of those passages is this: "Then those men, when they had seen the miracle that Jesus did, said, This is of a truth that prophet **that should come** into the world" (Fourth gospel 6:14). This was said by witnesses who saw Jesus feed five thousand men starting with only "five barley loaves, and two small fishes." Like those who saw Jesus raise a man from the dead and concluded "a great prophet is risen up among us," some of those who saw Jesus feed five thousand men concluded he was "that prophet that should come into the world."

In the second of those two passages, the possibility of Jesus being "the Prophet" was raised in response to his teaching:

"In the last day, that great *day* of the feast, Jesus stood and cried, saying, If any man thirst, let him come unto me, and drink. He that believeth on me, as the scripture hath said, out of his belly shall flow rivers of living water. (But this spake he of the Spirit, which they that believe on him should receive: for the Holy Ghost was not yet *given*; because that Jesus was not yet glorified.) Many of the people therefore, when they heard this saying, said, Of a truth this is **the Prophet**. Others said, This is the Christ. But some said, Shall Christ come out of Galilee?" (Fourth gospel 7:37-41).

"The Prophet."

"The Christ."

Some thought one thing, some believed another. However, what is missing is people who think "the Prophet" and "the Christ" could be the same person.

<u>"The Prophet"</u> *and* "the Christ"?

In Acts 3:19-26 we read the following:

> "Repent ye therefore, and be converted, that your sins may be blotted out, when the times of refreshing shall come from the presence of the Lord; And he shall send Jesus Christ, which before was preached unto you: Whom the heaven must receive until the times of restitution of all things, which God hath spoken by the mouth of all his holy prophets since the world began. For Moses truly said unto the fathers, A prophet shall the Lord your God raise up unto you of your brethren, like unto me; him shall ye hear in all things whatsoever he shall say unto you. And it shall come to pass, *that* every soul, which will not hear **that prophet**, shall be destroyed from among the people. Yea, and all the prophets from Samuel and those that follow after, as many as have spoken, have likewise foretold of **these days**. Ye are the children of the prophets, and of the covenant which God made with our fathers, saying unto Abraham, And in thy seed shall all the kindreds of the earth be blessed. Unto you first God, having raised up his Son Jesus, sent him to bless you, in turning away every one of you from his iniquities."

In John's day they were expecting someone *other than* "the Christ" – not instead of him, but *in addition to* him. [The passage above shows the prophecy about a prophet "like unto" Moses (aka "the Prophet" and "that prophet **that should come** into the world") referred to, and was fulfilled by, the <u>risen</u> Jesus. Acts 3 was written after Jesus rose from the dead. Thus, "foretold of **these days**" refers to the time after Jesus was raised, and the phrase "having raised up his Son Jesus" shows this also.] Before Jesus was raised, you would be hard-pressed to find anyone in scripture expressing the idea that one person would be both "the Prophet" and "the Christ." We know this idea was taught <u>after</u> Jesus rose from the dead, but John died long before that.

John did not have a post-resurrection view of Jesus. Thus, in order to understand his question, it must be considered in light of the thinking which prevailed at the time of his question.

In that era, it was assumed the roles of "the Christ" and "the Prophet" would be fulfilled by different men. Thus those who considered Jesus to be "the Christ" (as John did), would have been disinclined to think the Prophet spoken of by Moses might also refer to Jesus.

However, "among those that are born of women there is not a greater prophet than John the Baptist" (Lk 7:28). Thus, John would have been more likely than most to be open to correction and to pursue the truth.

[Jesus' words also reveal the prophet "like unto" Moses would not be "born of women" (for that prophet was going to be greater than John). Psalm 2:7 says, "Thou *art* my Son, this day have I begotten thee" and Acts 13:33 tells us this was fulfilled when God "raised up Jesus again" (cf. 13:30, "raised him from the dead"). The focus was not on when Jesus was born of Mary, but when he became "the **firstborn from the dead**" (Col 1:18). Similarly, Acts 3:19-24 links the prophecy about the prophet "like unto" Moses to Jesus <u>after</u> he rose from the dead.]

Given the evidence, what would an unbiased jury conclude:

(A) John's question had to do with Jesus being "the Christ," or
(B) John wondered if Jesus was the prophet "that should come" (because Jesus was called "a great prophet" when he raised a man from the dead, it led John to ask about this topic)?

If John wanted to know if Jesus was "he that should come" in addition to being "the Christ", then his question makes sense. Now let us see what we can learn from Jesus' response to John's question.

<u>"And in that same hour he cured many"</u>

In Luke 7:19-28 we read about John's question and Jesus' response:

"John calling *unto him* two of his disciples sent *them* to Jesus, saying, Art thou he **that should come**, or look we for another? When the men were come unto him, they said, John Baptist hath sent us unto thee, saying, Art thou he that should come, or look we for another? And in that same hour he cured many of *their* infirmities and plagues, and of evil spirits; and unto many *that were* blind he gave sight. Then Jesus answering said unto them, Go your way, and tell John what things ye have seen and heard; how that the blind see, the lame walk, the lepers are cleansed, the deaf hear, the dead are raised, to the poor the gospel is preached. And blessed is *he*, whosoever shall not be offended in me. And when the messengers of John were departed, he began to speak unto the people concerning John, What went ye out into the wilderness for to see? A reed shaken with the wind? But what went ye out for to see? A man clothed in soft raiment? Behold, they which are gorgeously appareled, and live delicately, are in kings' courts. But what went ye out for to see? A prophet? Yea, I say unto you, and much more than a prophet. This is *he*, of whom it is written, Behold, I send my messenger before thy face, which shall prepare thy way before thee. For I say unto you, Among those that are born of women there is not a greater prophet than John the Baptist."

At first, Jesus did not say anything. Instead, he did some things: "in that same hour he cured many of *their* infirmities and plagues, and of evil spirits; and unto many *that were* blind he gave sight" (Lk 7:21).

Since Jesus had already raised a man from the dead, those things were not done to prove his ability to work miracles. His actions here might even seem to be somewhat anti-climactic, in light of his raising the widow's son from the dead.

Why did Jesus, after hearing John's question, take the time to do what he did before he spoke a word in response to the question? Because his deeds were his answer!

Here again is Luke 7:21-23, the portion of the passage where we see what occurred after Jesus had heard John's question:

"And in that same hour he cured many of *their* infirmities and plagues, and of evil spirits; and unto many *that were* blind he gave sight. Then Jesus answering said unto them, Go your way, and tell John what things ye have seen and heard; how that the blind see, the lame walk, the lepers are cleansed, the deaf hear, the dead are raised, to the poor the gospel is preached. And blessed is *he*, whosoever shall not be offended in me."

Rather than simply give a verbal response to John's question, Jesus sent back a record of deeds for John to consider. What do you think Jesus wanted his cousin John to learn from this?

What Did John Know and When Did He Know It?

When John heard Jesus' answer to his question, he probably recalled words like, "Then the eyes of the blind shall be opened, and the ears of the deaf shall be unstopped" (Isa 35:5). Many passages of scripture had foretold of miraculous deeds and they spoke of the kind of works Jesus cited as evidence in his response to John.

Acts 10:43 says, "To him [Jesus] give all the prophets witness." Since "all the prophets" spoke of him, Jesus cited his works and John then had to consider that evidence in light of the testimony of God's word.

He would not be *only* "the Christ." Nor was he to be *only* "the Prophet." For example, Jesus would also be priest and king – a "high priest after the order of Melchisedec" (Heb 5:10) and "king of kings" (Rv 17:14, 19:16).

[Moreover, in order to be accurate, Jesus' response could not merely discuss the idea of him fulfilling multiple roles, because a prophecy is not fulfilled until it is fulfilled. Many prophecies (like the one that led the people of John's day to look for the "prophet **that should come**" (Fourth gospel 6:14)) were going to be fulfilled by Jesus only after he rose from the dead. "All the prophets" spoke of Jesus (Acts 10:43). However, their "witness" included things that would only be fulfilled after Jesus' resurrection. This was the case with the prophecy of "that prophet" (cf. Acts 3:22-26), and Jesus' response also had to take this into account.]

To understand the question John posed to Jesus, one must be sure to weigh the evidence that can shed light on John's frame of mind at that time.

The evidence indicates John, like others in his day, initially thought "the prophet" and "the Christ" were different people. Then he heard a report of people saying this about Jesus, "**a great prophet** is risen up among us" (Lk 7:16), and this led John to test his prior assumption by asking Jesus the question that is preserved for us in scripture.

The Conclusion to the Case of John's Question

Note two verses:

    (1) "Then those men, when they had seen the miracle that Jesus did, said, This is of a truth that prophet **that should come** into the world" (Fourth gospel 6:14), and

    (2) "Many of the people therefore, when they heard this [Jesus'] saying, said, Of a truth this is the Prophet" (Fourth gospel 7:40).

While many were not sure what to think about Jesus, those verses show that at least some people thought he might be "the prophet" they were expecting. However, the religious scholars and leaders led the people astray because they refused to believe the word of God, as Jesus himself noted when he said, "For had ye believed Moses, ye would have believed me: for he wrote of me" (Fourth gospel 5:46).

Although scripture reveals the people of Jesus' day saw "the Prophet" and "the Christ" as separate people, many people overlook this fact even though this truth was in scripture all along. If you missed it, then you can improve your Bible study method and, hopefully, you learned how important it is to give heed to "every word of God."

When John was asked about Jesus baptizing men, his reply included these notable comments:

    (A) "I am not the Christ, but that **I am sent before him**" (Fourth gospel 3:28); and

    (B) "he that cometh from above is above all" (Fourth gospel 3:31).

Those statements let us know how John viewed Jesus, and scripture never says he had second thoughts about those words or any of the other things he said about Jesus. Thus, there is no biblical reason to believe his question had anything to do with Jesus being "the Christ."

John's question makes sense if he wanted to know if Jesus was also going to fulfill the role of "that prophet that should come into the world" (in addition to fulfilling the prophecies regarding "the Christ"). Sadly, however, many preachers are led to explain away John's question by using excuses which are not related to the word of God. Why is this? It happens because schools train people to look to the writings of men for their answers to Bible questions. When people rely on that method they end up holding views that are founded on the beliefs of others.

What happens if people rely on commentaries to tell them how to view John's question? If those resources say John was asking if Jesus was "the Christ," then it will seem to be reasonable because *'that is what the experts say.'* If we buy their view, then from that point on our view of John's question will be skewed, and the confidence we put in men will prejudice our view of the passage. This shows the problem with relying on the teachings of men.

When we elect to put confidence in an author, teacher, or group, then we are going against the counsel of scripture and leaning on our own understanding (which is telling us to lean on *their* understanding).

"Rightly dividing the word of truth" (2 Tm 2:15), on the other hand, allows scripture to lead us to the correct understanding of John's question.

The end of the Case of John's Question

Chapter 5 – The Case of "Jesus Wept"

<u>The Shortest Verse</u>

In the eleventh chapter of the fourth gospel, the words "Jesus wept" comprise verse 35. Having just two words, it is the shortest verse in the Bible. Those words are in the passage that record Jesus' visit to the tomb of Lazarus, and some commonly taught ideas give people a false impression of this event, as will be shown.

Before proceeding, open a Bible and take a few moments to consider the verse in its original context. Make some notes on what you think scripture is teaching us in this passage. Then return to this study and see if the evidence found in scripture is able to correct some common erroneous assumptions about this verse.

###

The Case of "Jesus Wept"

<u>A Litmus Test for Truth</u>

The words "Jesus wept" occur in the passage that tells of Jesus' visit to the tomb of his friend Lazarus, which leads many to read various emotions into those words. Doing so causes people to say things like: *'his tears show us he was saddened by death and identified with all of those who have ever lost someone they loved'* or *'he cried because he shared Mary and Martha's burden of grief and he missed his friend Lazarus,'* etc. Is that really why he wept?

Visiting a tomb where mourners are weeping could easily move one to tears. Moreover, the grief of his friends Mary and Martha surely tugged at Jesus' heart. Yet we lean on our own understanding if we assume that is what caused him to weep. If we let scripture teach us to rightly divide the passage, then another view emerges:

"Now a certain *man* was sick, *named* Lazarus, of Bethany ... When Jesus heard *that*, he said, This sickness is not unto death, but for the glory of God, that the Son of God might be glorified thereby. Now Jesus loved Martha, and her sister, and Lazarus. When he had heard therefore that he was sick, he abode two days still in the same place where he was. Then after that saith he to *his* disciples, Let us go into Judea again ... Our friend Lazarus sleepeth; but I go, that I may awake him out of sleep. Then said his disciples, Lord, if he sleep, he shall do well. Howbeit Jesus spake of his death: but they thought that he had spoken of taking of rest in sleep. Then said Jesus unto them plainly, Lazarus is dead. And I am glad for your sakes that I was not there, to the intent ye may believe; nevertheless let us go unto him ... Then Martha, as soon as she heard that Jesus was coming, went and met him: but Mary sat *still* in the house. Then said Martha unto Jesus, Lord, if thou hadst been here, my brother had not died ... she went her way, and called Mary her sister ... Then when Mary was come where Jesus was, and saw him, she fell down at his feet, saying unto him, Lord, if thou hadst been here, my brother would not have died. When Jesus therefore saw her weeping, and the Jews also weeping which came with her, he groaned in the spirit, and was troubled, and said, Where have ye laid him? They said unto him, Lord, come and see. Jesus wept. Then said the Jews, Behold how he loved him! And some of them said, Could not this man, which opened the eyes of the blind, have caused that even this man should not have died?" (Fourth gospel 11:1-37)

With those words scripture establishes a litmus test for truth and this test lets us know "Jesus wept" cannot be compared to the tears we shed when we go to the funeral of a friend or loved one. Why not? Because unlike us when we attend a funeral, and unlike those who were mourning the death of Lazarus, Jesus was not there for a funeral – he was there to raise Lazarus from the dead!

A Time to Mourn?

The biblical evidence showing why "Jesus wept" and "groaned" and "was troubled" will be presented shortly. However, first it is important to learn how scripture disproves ideas like:

(A) *'Jesus wept over the death of a friend,'*
(B) *'Jesus wept as he joined with others in their grief,'*
(C) *'Jesus wept over the pain death causes,'* etc.

Those ideas fail the test of biblical scrutiny because Jesus knew he, and everyone there, would see Lazarus again in just a few moments. Jesus told the disciples, "Our friend Lazarus sleepeth; but I go, that I may awake him out of sleep." Then scripture says, "Jesus spake of his death." This lets us know Jesus planned to "go" and raise Lazarus from the dead. So, his knowledge of the upcoming miracle cannot be reconciled with the notion of him being sad and missing his friend.

Those who do not take account of the purpose of Jesus' visit make the same false assumption about his tears as did the Jews who saw him cry; "Jesus wept. Then said the Jews, Behold how he loved him!" The mourners *assumed* Jesus wept because of his love for Lazarus. Yet scripture reveals their inference was made in ignorance because they did not have all of the facts needed to discern the truth, such as the miracle Jesus planned to do.

Moreover, something else Jesus said should keep us from assuming *'Jesus wept because of the death of Lazarus.'* Scripture tells us, "Then said Jesus unto them plainly, Lazarus is dead. And I am **glad** for your sakes that I was not there, to the intent ye may believe," and his use of the word "glad" in talking about the death of Lazarus should arrest our attention! Jesus looked forward to what was about to occur because Lazarus' death and his raising of Lazarus from the dead would work together for the good of the disciples ["to the intent ye may believe"]. This alone ought to call into question the idea of Jesus weeping out of sadness because he missed Lazarus or because he identified with the mourners.

A Time to Weep?

"Jesus loved" Lazarus and called him "friend," but he did not cry:

- when he heard Lazarus was sick, nor
- when he said, "Lazarus is dead," nor
- when he met with Martha, nor
- when he met Mary and "saw her weeping, and the Jews also weeping which came with her."

Still, many assume identification with the mourner's grief is what led him to weep, even though the evidence does not fit that assumption. As the foregoing examples show, subjecting ideas to biblical scrutiny gives us a way to test the truth of biblical beliefs [by looking to see if the evidence in scripture justifies a given idea or contradicts it].

When Did Jesus Weep?

Considering why Jesus did not weep is fine, but the question remains, why did he weep? Jesus was not mourning the loss of his friend, nor did he shed tears when Martha and later Mary came to him weeping. So, what brought on his tears at the point where he finally wept?

Do a search on when Jesus shed tears and you will learn there was only one other time when Jesus publicly shed tears. In Luke 19, Jesus rode into "Jerusalem" on a "colt" and we are told:

> "when he was come near, he beheld the city, and wept over it, Saying, If thou hadst known, even thou, at least in this thy day, the things which belong unto thy peace! but now they are hid from thine eyes. For the days shall come upon thee, that thine enemies shall cast a trench about thee, and compass thee round, and keep thee in on every side, And shall lay thee even with the ground, and thy children within thee; and they shall not leave in thee one stone upon another; because thou knewest not the time of thy visitation" (Lk 19:41-44).

Why did Jesus weep on this occasion? It was over their ignorance of the time of the "visitation." This means they should have known it (i.e., it was foretold in scripture). They missed the truth and did not realize his presence in Jerusalem on that day was a fulfillment of prophesy. Their lack of knowledge about the things in God's word moved Jesus to tears at that point. Now, let us compare this to the "Jesus wept" passage. Why did Jesus weep at the tomb of Lazarus? What led him to weep __when__ he did? It was the response of the Jews to his question.

Focus on the sequence. Jesus asked, "Where have ye laid him? They said unto him, Lord, come and see. Jesus wept" (Fourth gospel 11:34-35). Why did their answer to his question move him to tears? Notice what came next: "Then said the Jews, Behold how he loved him! And some of them said, Could not this man, which opened the eyes of the blind, have caused that even this man should not have died?" (Fourth gospel 11:36-37). How does this help us see why "Jesus wept" in response to their "come and see" answer to his question?

A Necessary Detour

For a moment, let us leave the "Jesus wept" passage and consider a time when Jesus was surprised. Jesus once said, "I have not found so great faith, no, not in Israel" (Mt 8:10, Lk 7:9). What led him to say that? It was hearing the words of a centurion who had asked him to heal one of his servants (cf. Mt 8:5-13, Lk 7:2-10). Jesus was on his way to the centurion's house when he received this message:

"Lord, trouble not thyself: for I am not worthy that thou shouldest enter under my roof: Wherefore neither thought I myself worthy to come unto thee: but say in a word, and my servant shall be healed. For I also am a man set under authority, having under me soldiers, and I say unto one, Go, and he goeth; and to another, Come, and he cometh; and to my servant, Do this, and he doeth it. When Jesus heard these things, he marveled at him, and turned him about, and said unto the people that followed him, I say unto you, I have not found so great faith, no, not in Israel" (Lk 7:6-9).

The centurion's solid reasoning and his willingness to act accordingly had an impact on Jesus. The centurion and Jesus had something in common, for he said, "I **also** am a man set under authority." As a man "under authority," his orders were carried out because of the one who gave him his authority (Caesar). Because he recognized Jesus "also" was "a man set under authority," he concluded Jesus could, "say in a word" and his servant would "be healed." His reasoning teaches us how a person would necessarily be drawn to the same conclusion, if their reasoning is built on a consistent respect for truth.

A person seeking to help a sick child physically interacts with the child to provide aid, comfort, medication, etc. However, miracles overcome the things of this world, so physical interaction or nearness are not necessary. The authority to do miracles is not of this world. Therefore, any person who is "under authority" and doing miracles would not be bound by the rules of this world.

Follow the centurion's reasoning through to its logical conclusion and one must conclude Jesus would not have to be physically present to bless someone with a miracle. He would only need to give the order. Still, the centurion's logic is not what moved Jesus, it was his faith – he put that reasoning into action and sent word for Jesus not to come (and this showed he truly respected the power and authority of God).

Why Did Jesus Go to the Tomb?

Jesus did not go to Lazarus' tomb because he had to be close enough for Lazarus to hear him say, "Lazarus, come forth" (Fourth gospel 11:43). Lazarus was dead, so getting closer to his corpse was not going to increase the chance of him hearing Jesus' voice. But if Jesus had not gone there and raised Lazarus in the presence of his disciples, the miracle would not have produced the result Jesus intended.

Before he had even set out for Bethany on that day, Jesus told the disciples why he was going there. "Lazarus is dead. And I am glad **for your sakes** that I was not there, **to the intent ye may believe**; nevertheless let us go unto him" (Fourth gospel 11:14-15). Thus his intent in raising Lazarus was not, first and foremost, to stop the tears of Martha, Mary, and the other mourners, nor was it to give Lazarus more time in this world. It was so those disciples would believe! Jesus raised Lazarus in the presence of his disciples for their benefit, but those disciples were not the only ones who witnessed the miracle.

Jesus had not yet reached the town when Mary and those who were with her went out to meet him. Then we are told:

"Jesus therefore saw her weeping, and the Jews also weeping which came with her, he groaned in the spirit, and was troubled, And said, Where have ye laid him? They said unto him, Lord, come and see. Jesus wept. Then said the Jews, Behold how he loved him! And some of them said, Could not this man, which opened the eyes of the blind, have caused that even this man should not have died? Jesus therefore again groaning in himself cometh to the grave" (Fourth gospel 11:33-38).

When Jesus asked, "Where have ye laid him?" how should the Jews have responded? Their words prove they knew he had the power to stop death. This knowledge should have led them to say, 'you do not need to go there, just say a word and he shall be raised.' But while their words prove they knew Jesus represented an authority that was not of this world, they did not follow this to its logical conclusion and act in faith (as the centurion had done).

"No, not in Israel"

Faced with a miracle worker, the centurion said, *'no need to come.'* Faced with the same man, the Jews said, "Lord, come and see." The centurion certainly had less data to go on than they did. First off, they had a heritage built on the word of God and he did not. Also, the Jews specifically referred to Jesus opening the eyes of the blind, and they probably were aware of many of his other miracles as well.

From the early days of Jesus' ministry, the people of Jerusalem knew of his miracles; "When he was in Jerusalem at the Passover, in the feast *day*, many believed in his name, when they saw the miracles which he did" (Fourth gospel 2:23). In addition to the miracles themselves, even the quantity of them made an impression: "Many of the people believed on him, and said, When Christ cometh, will he do **more** miracles than these which this man hath done?" (Fourth gospel 7:31)

There is no telling what miracles of Jesus the Jews at the tomb of Lazarus had heard about (or that may have been witnessed by them or a relative). Beyond the miracles, they had other reasons to know Jesus had been sent by God. In all of Jesus' teaching and in all of his confrontations with religious leaders, he honored the authority of God and those who were obedient to God knew this was so.

One time when Jesus was teaching in the temple, we are told:

"the Jews marveled, saying, How knoweth this man letters, having never learned? Jesus answered them, and said, My doctrine is not mine, but his that sent me. **If any man will do his will, he shall <u>know</u> of the doctrine, whether it be of God, or whether I speak of myself**" (Fourth gospel 7:15-17).

Even the men who were sent by the religious leaders to seize Jesus on one occasion (cf. Fourth gospel 7:32) recognized the teaching of Jesus was very different. When they returned without him, the chief priests and Pharisees asked, "Why have ye not brought him? The officers answered, Never man spake like this man" (Fourth gospel 7:45-46).

In spite of knowing what Jesus had done and taught, when he asked, "Where have ye laid him?" the Jews responded, "Lord, come and see" – and only then did Jesus weep! It was a sad moment, but it may be wrong to assume he wept because of *sadness* over their lack of faith. People shed tears for lots of reasons. Some weep for joy at weddings. Indignation moves others to tears at injustices like human trafficking. So, let us take another look to see if scripture has more to say on this.

Overcoming the Language Barrier

The writers of scripture did not write in English. This is why those who use an English Bible can benefit by looking at the Hebrew and Greek words that were used by the writers of scripture. Case in point, in the "Jesus wept" passage the words "groaned" and "groaning" describe Jesus' reaction ("he groaned in the spirit, and was troubled"), *before* he asked, "Where have ye laid him?" After the Jews acknowledged Jesus had the power to prevent death, it says, "Jesus <u>therefore</u> again groaning in himself cometh to the grave" (Fourth gospel 11:38). Yet, if one relates those verses to other verses having the word "groan," they might get the wrong impression if they are not diligent.

Several Greek words were translated as "groan." The one translated as "groaned" and "groaning" in the "Jesus wept" passage was used only three other times in scripture, and none of those times was it translated as "groaned" or "groaning." Twice it was translated as "straightly charged," and once as "murmured against" (Mt 9:30, Mk 1:43, 14:5). The definition of this word includes: to be angry, to be moved with indignation, and to sternly charge.

Both verses where the word was translated as "straightly charged" tell of Jesus giving an order to men he had healed, who then went out and directly disobeyed him (Mt 9:30-31, Mk 1:43-45). This word was used only other time when, "some that had indignation within themselves" had "murmured against" a woman who gave Jesus an expensive gift (Mk 14:4-5). In this verse "indignation" is linked to the word translated as "groaned" and "groaning" in the "Jesus wept" passage, and we need to take account of this if we want to be led by the word of God.

The Conclusion of the Case of "Jesus Wept"

"Jesus wept" right after he heard the Jews' response to his question, and scripture indicates it was their ignorance and/or lack of faith that moved him to tears at that moment. The greatest public miracle of his earthly ministry is, arguably, the raising of Lazarus. Jesus knew it was going to happen before he went to Lazarus' tomb and we are told why he did it. The LORD said, "he that hath my word, <u>let him speak my word faithfully</u>" (Jer 23:28). But instead of letting God's word speak for itself, men who think they can say it better prefer to put it in their own words. When people say things like, *'Jesus wept over the death of his friend,'* they are not being faithful to God's word (whether they know it or not).

The end of the Case of "Jesus Wept"

Chapter 6 – The Case of God's Gift

<u>A Familiar Verse</u>

"For God so loved the world, that he gave his only begotten Son, that whosoever believeth in him should not perish, but have everlasting life" (Fourth gospel 3:16). Most churchgoers have heard this verse quoted many times. However, familiarity with a passage should not keep us from doing our due diligence (a temptation more likely to occur when it comes to frequently quoted verses).

Get your Bible and read the verse in its context. Apply your normal study method and write down your thoughts about what you think the verse is saying. Afterwards, come back to this study and see if your current method of assessing truth on biblical issues led you to miss insights on the verse that God's word has to offer.

###

The Case of God's Gift

"For God So Loved"

"For God so loved the world, that he gave his only begotten Son, that whosoever believeth in him should not perish, but have everlasting life" (Fourth gospel 3:16). Two ideas are often emphasized when teachers cite this verse. Almost without exception they will say something like, *'the verse teaches God loved the world so much that it moved him to send Jesus to die for the world.'* They also typically add, *'this tells us God's love is unconditional.'* A version of one or both of those ideas will usually be included when this verse is taught in churches today.

If "For God so loved the world" is the most well-known Bible verse in our era and *if* it is routinely taught incorrectly, then this might make it the most misunderstood verse of scripture (in quantity terms at least). If this is true, then it raises another question: why is this verse not taught correctly? There is no reason to consider the second question unless scripture can show the verse is routinely misunderstood and taught incorrectly, so this is what we will look at first.

God's Unconditional Love?

A Better Bible Study Method, Book One offered these comments on the verse in question:

> "For God so loved the world, that he gave his only begotten Son, that whosoever believeth in him should not perish, but have everlasting life." When this verse is quoted, it is common to hear comments like, *'This speaks of God's unconditional love for you.'* But why would people allow this claim to go unchallenged when it is contrary to the plain reading of the text? To say the verse informs everyone about God's unconditional love for them is to twist the verse beyond recognition – since it is a conditional statement and the condition is clearly stated in the verse.
>
> Should a person conclude the blessing of "not perish, but have everlasting life" applies to those who do *not* "believe in him?" Not according to the verse. We are not talking about whatever scripture says elsewhere, but about faithfully communicating what this verse actually says. It tells us the reason God "gave his only begotten Son" was "**that**" those who meet the condition ("believeth in him") should "not perish." So, the condition is vital to the verse.

People may get various insights from the verse, but it does not say God's love is unconditional. So, linking the idea of unconditional love to the verse undermines the authority of the words of the verse itself.

<u>What about the "Whosoever?"</u>

Many assume the word "whosoever" makes the verse unconditional. While many claim the word "whosoever" means the verse is directed to everyone without condition, what happens if one puts this claim to the test? Consider the following sample of five verses where the word "whosoever" was used:

- "I [Aaron] said unto them, Whosoever hath any gold, let them break *it* off" (Ex 32:24);
- "Speak unto Aaron, saying, Whosoever *he be* of thy seed in their generations that hath *any* blemish, let him not approach to offer the bread of his God" (Lv 21:17);
- "Whosoever heareth these sayings of mine [Jesus], and doeth them, I will liken him unto a wise man, which built his house upon a rock" (Mt 7:24);
- "Take heed therefore how ye hear: for whosoever hath, to him shall be given; and whosoever hath not, from him shall be taken even that which he seemeth to have" (Lk 8:18);
- "Whosoever shall confess that Jesus is the Son of God, God dwelleth in him, and he in God" (1 Jo 4:15).

Does "whosoever" refer to any and every person without condition?

<u>Let Scripture Light the Way</u>

If we want to learn the meaning of a word in scripture, we should be careful not to let the opinions of others prejudice our view of scripture. Rather, we should let scripture teach us the meaning of the words, phrases, and word pictures used in the Bible. If we let scripture show us how to view the word "whosoever" here is what we can learn from the verses cited above:

- "I [Aaron] said unto them, Whosoever hath any gold, let them break *it* off" – In this verse the word "whosoever" <u>introduced a condition</u> that defined a specific subset of people (those with "any gold");
- "Speak unto Aaron, saying, Whosoever *he be* of thy seed in their generations that hath *any* blemish..." – "Whosoever" cannot include everyone in this case, for not everyone was of Aaron's seed. Rather, the word <u>introduced a condition</u> that defined a subset of people among the seed of Aaron;

- "Whosoever heareth these sayings of mine, and doeth them..." – "Whosoever" refers only to those who meet the condition (i.e., hears Jesus' sayings and does them) and it excludes everyone else;
- "whosoever hath, to him shall be given; and whosoever hath not..." – It is impossible for everybody to be in both groups! Here the word "whosoever" was used twice in order to define two distinct groups, based on two distinct conditions (the condition "hath" defines one group and "hath not" defines a different group);
- "Whosoever shall confess that Jesus is the Son of God..." – Here only those who "confess that Jesus is the Son of God" are included, since this is the specified condition.

In each verse the word "whosoever" introduced a condition. So, those who claim "whosoever" makes a verse unconditional are leaning on their own understanding and ignoring biblical evidence. A quick look shows similar terms like, "whoso," "whomsoever," "whatsoever," and "soever," are all tied to a condition:

- "Whoso *is* wise, and will observe these *things*, even they shall understand the loving-kindness of the LORD" (Ps 107:43);
- "he [Judas] that betrayed him [Jesus] gave them a sign, saying, Whomsoever I shall kiss, that same is he" (Mt 26:48);
- "Every beast, every creeping thing, and every fowl, *and* whatsoever creepeth upon the earth, after their kinds, went forth out of the ark" (Gn 8:19);
- "And he [Jesus] said unto them, In what place soever ye enter into a house, there abide till ye depart..." (Mk 6:10).

In the Bible those words always designate a grouping based on some condition(s) or trait(s) that define who or what is included in the group being discussed. The word "whosoever" appears 163 times in the KJV and it **always** introduces a condition or set of conditions. It is not specifying who can or cannot meet the condition. All it does is define a set (and the set includes those who meet or have already met the condition(s) that are specified in the verse or passage).

How to Verify the Meaning of a Word

Now we will venture beneath the surface data to further establish how scripture itself clarifies the meaning of the words we find in the Bible. It takes a little time to look into the words, but knowing how the writers of scripture used a word can reveal things we might otherwise miss.

Our English Bible is a translation of the Hebrew or Greek words used by the writers of scripture. When we are uncertain about the meaning of a word or passage, those Hebrew or Greek words can help us to clear up or prevent misunderstandings *even if we do not speak those languages*. How? By looking at other verses that have the same word and letting scripture's use of a word teach us things about that word.

While this may sound difficult, it is surprisingly easy to do thanks to a numbering system that helps us identify those words. A tool called Strong's Concordance has assigned different numbers to the Greek and Hebrew words. This lets us see how each word was translated in every verse where it was used.

For example, if three Greek words are translated by a single English word, then the three different Strong's numbers for those words call our attention to this fact. Or if we are unsure of the proper meaning of a particular word in our Bible, then the number of the original word lets us identify all of the other verses where the same word was used – and we can gain insight about a word by seeing how it is used in other verses. [Numerous free online Bible study tools make it easy to access the Strong's number for any word.]

That said, only one Greek word number will be cited in this case, and it will show how scripture itself can establish the meaning of a word. Seeing how a word was used in scripture helps us to understand what was written, and the time it takes to look at the original words is well worth it. [The format $^{G\#\#\#\#}$ will be used so you can easily follow the Strong's number of the Greek word being discussed.]

So?

Many English words have multiple meanings. If we associate a word with the wrong meaning when reading scripture, it will skew our view of God's word until we realize and correct our mistake. The word "so" has multiple meanings and here are a few examples:

- indicates a quantity; i.e., a large amount or extreme degree
  (he *so* loves the smell of coffee; he has *so* much money);
- indicates a quality; i.e., the way a thing is or was done
  (he takes his coffee like *so*; it happened just *so*)
- consequently, therefore
  (he had too much coffee, *so* he is unable to sleep)
- in order that
  (he drinks coffee *so* he can stay awake)
- indeed, certainly
  (he does *so* drink coffee)

In these two examples the word "so" refers to a quantity:

- "When Jesus heard *it*, he marveled, and said to them that followed, Verily I say unto you, I have not found so great faith, no, not in Israel" (Mt 8:10);
- "his disciples say unto him, Whence should we have so much bread in the wilderness, as to fill so great a multitude?" (Mt 15:33).

In these two examples the word "so" refers to a quality:

- "But those things, which God before had shewed by the mouth of all his prophets, that Christ should suffer, he hath so fulfilled" (Acts 3:18);
- "they which run in a race run all, but one receiveth the prize? So run, that ye may obtain" (1 Cor 9:24).

In the four verses above, the word "so" translates two Greek words, one refers to quantity, the other refers to quality. Quantity and quality are different ideas. If we assign the wrong meaning to the word "so," we will misunderstand scripture. Looking at the Strong's number for the word which was translated as "so" gives us an easy way to verify the correct meaning of the word, because quantity and quality were expressed by different Greek words (with different word numbers).

In the verses just cited, the phrase "so fulfilled" (Acts 3:18) does not refer to the amount of fulfillment. Rather, it refers to the manner in which "those things" were fulfilled. Likewise, the phrase "so run" (1 Cor 9:24) was not urging a lot of running. It referred to how one runs and urged running in a way that resulted in victory. In those verses the word "so" is translating the Greek word with the number [G3779] and this word always refers to a quality. For example, "if then God so [G3779] clothe the grass" (Lk 12:28) and "for so [G3779] is the will of God" (1 Pt 2:15) are speaking about the quality of the design that is seen in the grass and a quality of God's will, not the quantity of those things.

Let Scripture Light the Way Once Again

"Let every one of you in particular so [G3779] love his wife even as himself" (Eph 5:33) refers to the way a husband should "love his wife," not how much love he should send her way. Similarly, "Beloved, if God so [G3779] loved us, we ought also to love one another" (1 Jo 4:11) is a reference to a quality, not a quantity – the "beloved" were urged to "love one another" just as God loved them – and this refers to **how** God loved them, *not how much*.

In those verses the context lets us know what meaning is attached to the word "so," but this is not always the case. Sometimes the context does not clearly establish whether the word "so" refers to a quantity (intensity) or a quality (manner). However, today there is no reason to be confused because we can verify if the word "so" is translating a Greek word that refers to quantity or quality.

The easiest way to confirm scripture's use of word number G3779 is to look at the first ten verses where this word appears:

- "the birth of Jesus Christ was **on this wise** G3779" (Mt 1:18);
- **"thus** G3779 it is written by the prophet" (Mt 2:5);
- **"thus** G3779 it becometh us to fulfil all righteousness" (Mt 3:15);
- "great *is* your reward in heaven: for **so** G3779 persecuted they the prophets" (Mt 5:12);
- "Let your light **so** G3779 shine before men, that they may see your good works" (Mt 5:16);
- "Whosoever therefore shall break one of these least commandments, and shall teach men **so** G3779" (Mt 5:19);
- "if ye salute your brethren only, what do ye more *than others*? do not even the publicans **so** G3779?" (Mt 5:47);
- **"After this manner** G3779 therefore pray ye" (Mt 6:9);
- "if God **so** G3779 clothe the grass of the field" (Mt 6:30);
- "whatsoever ye would that men should do to you, do ye even **so** G3779 to them" (Mt 7:12).

Anyone who looks at just the first ten uses of word number G3779 will have to admit this Greek word refers to a quality, not to a quantity.

How Much? Or How?

The foregoing evidence exposes a view of the word "so" that leads many to misunderstand the phrase, "God so G3779 loved the world." When we are taught a verse means one thing, but scripture can prove otherwise, it proves those who unknowingly teach the erroneous view have relied on a method of assessing truth which is not reliable.

An interlinear KJV Bible has a literal translation of the words and word number G3779 will be translated as 'in this manner,' 'thus,' etc. because this **is** what the word means. This is confirmed by the way it was used elsewhere in scripture. Moreover, the New Testament writers had Greek words to use if they wanted to designate a quantity or intensity, and they did so many times. (Search for words like "much," "many," "exceeding(ly)," or "great(ly)," for examples of such verses.) However, none of those Greek words appear in the verse in question.

If we bought into the false view of "for God so loved the world," then we need to change our method of assessing truth on biblical issues. When we have believed something and it turns out not to be true, we need to ask, *'why did I believe the Bible said something it never said?'* Gaining a right understanding of "for God so loved the world" is good, but if we were wrong about this verse, then we must also figure out why we thought the verse said something it does not say.

Do Not Pass the Blame

Since the word "so" has multiple meanings, quantity (i.e., *'so much'*) is one possible meaning. But why would a person assume that was the right meaning? With all the Bible study tools available in our day, there really is no good reason for associating the wrong meaning with the word "so" in this verse.

Those who assign a wrong meaning of the word "so" cannot blame the Bible translators, since "so" is a perfectly proper way to translate word number [G3779]. While people can read a wrong meaning into the word "so," scripture always indicated the correct meaning of the word "so" in the phrase, "for God so loved the world."

"Every word of God *is* pure: he *is* a shield unto them that put their trust in him. Add thou not unto his words, lest he reprove thee, and thou be found a liar" (Prv 30:5-6). In this case, scripture can correct us if we have a wrong view of the word "so" and all it takes is a simple word search. Moreover, the Bible offers other evidence against the common misconceptions about the verse in question.

Still More Evidence

Now let us consider what scripture says immediately before and after the words, "God so loved the world":

> "as Moses lifted up the serpent in the wilderness, even so must the Son of man be lifted up: That whosoever believeth in him should not perish, but have eternal life. For God so loved the world, that he gave his only begotten Son, that whosoever believeth in him should not perish, but have everlasting life. For God sent not his Son into the world to condemn the world; but that the world through him might be saved. He that believeth on him is not condemned: but he that believeth not is condemned already, because he hath not believed in the name of the only begotten Son of God" (Fourth gospel 3:14-18).

The condition "whosoever believeth in him" appears twice (before it shows up in verse 16, it shows up in verse 15). Unless one reads only verse 16 or hears it quoted out of context, it is clear the author meant to focus his readers on the condition since he repeated it. In addition, verse 15 has to do with **how** people get saved. When "Moses lifted up the serpent in the wilderness," it provided a means by which men who had been bitten by a serpent could be saved (cf. Nm 21:7-9). Also in verse 17, the words "that the world through him might be saved" refer to **how** the world "might be saved" (i.e., "through him").

The word "so" in verse 14 refers to the manner in which "the Son of man" would "be lifted up" and this is the very same Greek word (^{G3779}) translated "so" in verse 16. Thus, the way the word "so" was used in verse 14 testifies against those who falsely claim the same word has a completely different meaning in verse 16.

Look for Similar Verses

Finally, if we want to see if our belief about a passage is true, then we should see if the same idea is expressed elsewhere in scripture. If "for God so loved the world, that he gave his only begotten Son" is about the way God expressed his love, then this idea will line up with other verses on the same topic. Do any other verses explicitly tell us how God expressed his love? Yes. "In this was manifested the love of God toward us, because that God sent his only begotten Son into the world, that we might live through him" (1 Jo 4:9).

"In this was manifested the love of God" refers to the way "the love of God" was expressed. How was it "manifested?" "God sent his only begotten Son into the world" – this is how God's love was expressed. Why did God do it? "That we might live through him" (and the "we" is those who believe in Jesus, the condition spelled out in all the verses where phrases like "whosoever believeth in him" appear).

Moreover, the term "God so loved" was only used in one other verse: "Beloved, if God so ^{G3779} loved us, we ought also to love one another" (1 Jo 4:11). This verse details an obligation for the "beloved"/"brethren" (cf. 1 Jo 3:13, 4:7), and it was not about the *amount of* love they "ought" to have for "one another." Here is 1 John 4:11 in context:

"Beloved, let us love one another: for love is of God; and every one that loveth is born of God, and knoweth God. He that loveth not knoweth not God; for God is love. In this was manifested the love of God toward us, because that God sent his only begotten Son into the world, that we might live through him. Herein is love, not that we loved God, but that he loved us, and sent his Son *to be* the propitiation for our sins. Beloved, if God so loved us, we ought also to love one another" (1 Jo 4:7-11).

Here too, scripture provides a check against a commonly promoted misunderstanding of the phrase "so loved."

Is It a Big Deal?

Because correction requires us to admit we have been wrong, many people downplay their mistakes by saying things like, *'it's no big deal,'* *'what difference does it make,'* *'it doesn't really matter,'* etc. Doing so serves to downplay one's misunderstanding of God's word by acting as if the truth is sometimes unimportant. Acting as if false beliefs are inconsequential is something people do to avoid having to deal with a bigger issue: errors are symptoms, they indicate and are caused by a false measure of truth.

Think about the common teaching of "for God so loved the world" and ask yourself if switching the meaning of the word "so" from a quality to a quantity is no big deal or a critical mistake? While many problems are caused by adopting a *'God loves you so much'* view of the verse, let us look at just one such problem and, hopefully, this will show why it is never a good to ignore truth in order to hold on to error.

Consider the focus of the verse. If the verse means, *'God loves you so much that if you were the only person in the world he still would have sent his son to die for you,'* then where is the focus? It is on you (i.e., *'God's love for you is so great he just had to rescue you'*). But is this what the verse means? No. If we do not twist the words to fit the teachings of men, where is the focus of the verse? It is on the gift! "For God **so** loved the world, that he gave his only begotten Son" puts the focus on Jesus, not us. Seeing ourselves at the center of the verse and thinking it revolves around us boosts our ego. While such themes may 'win friends and influence people', those people will be influenced in a way that inflates their self-esteem at the expense of the truth.

When the verse is understood correctly it presents Jesus as the way a person can experience the love of God. This aligns with the words of Jesus, "I am the way, the truth, and the life: no man cometh unto the Father, but by me" (Fourth gospel 14:6). The condition set forth in the verse ("believeth in him") makes it clear that believing in Jesus is **how** one can "have everlasting life." Here too, the proper understanding of the passage is confirmed by other verses like, "He that believeth on the Son hath everlasting life: and he that believeth not the Son shall not see life" (Fourth gospel 3:36) and "He that hath the Son hath life; *and* he that hath not the Son of God hath not life" (1Jo 5:12).

When "God so loved the world..." is rightly understood, it is consistent with what is said elsewhere in scripture. But the harmony is ruined if we say a conditional statement is unconditional or if we put ourselves at the center of a verse instead of realizing how it focused on Jesus. If that is not enough to make this a big deal, consider what this says about the Bible study practices of today.

Being Faithful to God's Word

In Jeremiah 23:28 the LORD said, "he that hath my word, let him speak my word faithfully," and there is no reason to think this admonition is less important now. We should never say scripture says something it does not say. So, the next time someone talks to you about *'God's unconditional love'*, ask them to cite a verse that has no condition.

One way to avoid being deceived by teachings that are not faithful to scripture is to heed this advice: "Prove all things; hold fast that which is good" (1 Th 5:21). Put this to the test on "for God so loved the world." If a teacher says, *'that verse teaches God loves you'* or *'that means God loves you, he always has and always will,'* what would you see if you compare their words to the words of the verse? Besides the fact the words are strikingly different, did you catch the tense change?

The word "loved" is in the past tense because it referred to something that already occurred (i.e., when God "gave his only begotten Son"). Notice "gave" is also past tense. The verse says "loved," not *'loves,'* and we should not reword scripture to make it conform to our beliefs. The benefits of God's gift are still available to anyone who satisfies the condition ("believeth in him"). However, the past tense was used because the verse told of a love that had already been expressed through a gift already given. For the same reason the past tense also shows up in this verse, "In this was manifested the love of God toward us, because that God sent his only begotten Son into the world, that we might live through him" (1 Jo 4:9). The terms "was manifested" and "sent" let us know the manifestation of God's love occurred prior to the time the verse was written.

Bumper Sticker Theology

'Warm-and-fuzzy' may sell bumper stickers, but it usually fails the test of scripture. *'God loves everybody'* is an idea promoted frequently by teachers, broadcasts, and books. Yet, if it is right for someone to say *'God loves you'* to anyone and everyone, then why did Jesus and the apostles not do so?

Scripture records many times when Jesus, and later the apostles, spoke to crowds. Not once did they ever declare *'God loves you'* to those in attendance! Therefore, if we were to judge using the method of Jesus and the apostles as our measure, what would we conclude? We would have to conclude making indiscriminate and unconditional public declarations of *'God loves you'* is a practice that is **not** in line with the public messages delivered by Jesus and the apostles.

Moreover, if a verse does not support the *'God loves everybody'* idea, what do we do? Can we pretend verses like Psalm 5:5 do not exist? In speaking of the LORD it says, "thou hatest all workers of iniquity." When ideas are promoted which are contrary to the whole counsel of God's word, it undermines the effect and authority of the word of God.

Also, Jesus once said, "Then will I profess unto them, I never knew you: depart from me, ye that work iniquity" (Mt 7:23). Does this suggest those workers of iniquity were once loved by Jesus, but later fell out of favor? If not, then it cannot be right for preachers to say things like, *'God loves you, he always has and he always will'* as if this is true for anybody and everybody, regardless of if they "work iniquity" or not.

Bad Methods Corrupt Good Data

Scripture **is** profitable for correction. It can set us straight, if we will submit to the authority of God's word. Yet a false view of the verse in question is not the only thing we need to correct. Health problems are best resolved by dealing with the root cause rather than suppressing the symptoms. In the same way, we need to deal with the cause of our false beliefs.

If our method of assessing truth has led us to think something is true when it is not true, then we need to correct both what we believed (the false idea) and why we believed it (the error-prone methodology). Unless we deal with the flaw in our method of assessing truth, our faulty approach to God's word will lead us to fall prey to other errors.

If biblical evidence can prove the popular teachings about "for God so loved the world" do not come from scripture, then those ideas are founded on something else. It is this problem (i.e., relying on a source other than God's word) that must be dealt with if the body of Christ is going to be best served.

The difference between quality and quantity is no little matter. So why do so many who claim to know Greek still teach this verse incorrectly, especially since the Greek is *not* ambiguous?

The difference between conditional and unconditional is also not a little matter. So why do many teachers link this verse to the notion of 'unconditional love' when the verse itself has an explicit condition?

Of course, holding a wrong belief about "for God so loved the world" does not mean everything else a person believes is wrong. However, when a verse as well-known as this verse is routinely misunderstood and/or misrepresented by those who read the Bible, it suggests the source of the problem has a common link. That link is the practice of promoting the teachings of men.

Think Inside the Book

We do not need to understand everything about a passage to see if an idea fails the test of scripture. When we are considering any idea, belief, or teaching we should ask ourselves things like: Is it contrary to anything in God's word? Does it line up with the life and the words of Jesus? Would it apply to the apostles? In other words, we should get in the habit of letting scripture serve as a litmus test for truth.

The term 'think outside the box' is used to encourage thinking that is not limited by assumptions which may be untrue. This kind of thinking is needed for us to receive biblical correction, because we have to be willing to have our assumptions challenged. Yet people can also be creative in finding ways to make scripture seem to mean what they want it to say. So, we need to make sure we do not deceive ourselves with such thinking. How can we avoid falling into that trap?

Think inside the book!

Obviously, the book in this case is the Bible. The point is to remind us to make sure our standard for assessing truth on biblical issues is what God's word has to say on the matter (and not what is said by our favorite teacher(s) or some group).

The Conclusion to the Case of God's Gift

"For God so loved the world, that he gave his only begotten Son, that whosoever believeth in him should not perish, but have everlasting life." This tells us **what God did** ("gave his only begotten Son") and **why God did it** ("that whosoever believeth in him should not perish, but have everlasting life"). Therefore, telling people the verse means *'God loves everyone,' 'God loves you so much and he loves you just the way you are,'* etc. turns them away from the verse's true meaning.

If people judged teachings only by what scripture says, then the most commonly taught errors would be rejected. When we let the words of scripture lead us to the truth (and note the context so we do not read a wrong meaning into them), then the truth presents itself.

The real danger of the teachings of men is their power to blind people to the truths in the word of God. As this case proved, truths that are set forth in the plain text of scripture can become hidden to us when we base our understanding of scripture on the teachings of men.

Not long before his death, Jesus told his disciples:

"Greater love hath no man than this, that a man lay down his life for his friends. Ye are my friends, if ye do whatsoever I command you" (Fourth gospel 15:13-14).

Notice two things:

(A) Jesus indicated he was laying down his life for his friends, and
(B) he told them what it takes to be his friend.

Scripture does not suggest everybody is going to be a friend of Jesus and we need to take account of this fact.

Proverbs 30:5-6 says:

"Every word of God *is* pure: he *is* a shield unto them that put their trust in him. Add thou not unto his words, lest he reprove thee, and thou be found a liar."

This passage is repeated here because it points to the right standard and it warns us against being careless and/or getting creative when it comes to God's word.

A final word on the problem of assuming God is unconditional in his grace, mercy, love, etc. The LORD said, "[I] will be gracious to whom I will be gracious, and will shew mercy on whom I will shew mercy" (Ex 33:19). To/on "whom I will" is a condition, and Romans 9:15-18 proves this limiting factor still applies. Also, Proverbs 14:26 says "In the fear of the LORD *is* strong confidence." But, people have nothing to fear if the LORD accepts everyone unconditionally, and if fear is eliminated, then people are cut-off from the benefits of the "the fear of the LORD."

The end of the Case of God's Gift

Chapter 7 – Who Says So?

"Cease, my son, to hear the instruction *that causeth*
to err from the words of knowledge" (Prv 19:27).

"Unjust in the Least"

The five case studies have shown the benefits of using a method of assessing truth on biblical issues that is in accord with the counsel of God's word. The real test, however, comes when biblical correction confronts us on a subject or a practice which is near and dear to us, for then the temptation is to take offense at the truth.

When people are confronted with evidence that calls into question something they thought was true, they can avoid dealing with those facts by giving themselves an excuse to ignore them. Sometimes people do this is by declaring a subject to be a minor issue or a secondary matter, while saying they prefer to focus on major issues or more important matters. But is it really okay to ignore God's word on issues *we deem* to be minor?

In Luke 16:1-13 when he spoke "unto his disciples," Jesus tied the concept of faithfulness to the little things with these words, "he that is faithful in that which is least is faithful also in much" (v 10). In calling his disciple's attention to things men consider "the least," Jesus did not stop there. Jesus gave no wiggle room for those who are tempted to downplay things *they* deem to be the little things or minor issues – for he also said, "he that is unjust in the least is also unjust in much," and that does not suggest it is okay for men to disregard God's word on issues *they* consider to be minor or irrelevant.

Integrity is rooted in consistency. A consistent respect for the truth begins with a willingness to submit to the authority of scripture on every issue. This cannot change simply because we think something is a minor issue. Some will act as if they can be faithful in *'the majors'* while they ignore what scripture says on issues which they deem to be *'the minors.'* However, the words of Jesus indicate being unfaithful to the truth in little matters means it is also occurring on larger issues.

When we are challenged by something in scripture, do we honor God if we brush aside the matter and say it is not a 'major' issue? Instead of looking for an excuse to ignore details in scripture when they are contrary to something we believe, we need to strive to be consistent in our regard for the authority of God's word.

The Authority of Scripture

James 2:10-11 emphasizes the unity and the authority of God's word:

> "For whosoever shall keep the whole law, and yet offend in one
> *point*, he is guilty of all. For he [God] that said, Do not commit
> adultery, said also, Do not kill. Now if thou commit no adultery,
> yet if thou kill, thou art become a transgressor of the law."

Why is a person "guilty of all" if they "offend in one *point*" only? Sadly, those who misunderstand this idea will often use the term *'sin is sin'* (which falsely implies all sins are equally bad), because they assume this verse justifies simplistically lumping together all offenses against God or others. But it does not. Rather, the passage actually highlights this principle: God's word comes from God.

James 2:11 has this line of reasoning: "he that said" *'x'* "said also" *'y'.* "He" must refer to God because it was "God" (Ex 20:1) who said "thou shalt not kill" (Ex 20:13) and "thou shalt not commit adultery" (Ex 20:14). Thus, the 'he who said this also said that' line of reasoning tells us a man who ignores what God said in one area of the law is "guilty of all" because he has shown disrespect for the authority behind the law. God stands behind every word of God, so an offense on any point is an act against the authority of God. This is the focus of the passage.

Although the verses in James explicitly mention the "law", the same logic would apply to anything else God has said. What God said in "the whole law" has the same authority as any other words of God because they come from the same source. Since God is the source of God's word, we must be consistent in our regard for scripture if we truly want to honor God.

"God, who at sundry times and in divers manners spake in time past unto the fathers by the prophets" (Heb 1:1) and "all scripture *is* given by inspiration of God" (2 Tm 3:16) are just two of the verses that tell us God is the source of scripture. Those verses also let us know the authority of God's word is not diminished when it is faithfully communicated through the mouth or pen of a man (because the source of the words is not the messenger, it is God).

The Integrity of Our Method

Jesus told the Jews of his day, "For had ye believed Moses, ye would have believed me: for he wrote of me" (Fourth gospel 5:46). What does this tell us about the Jews? It proves they were deceived. How so? Did the Jews of that day *think* they believed Moses? Surely, they did.

But *thinking* they believed Moses did not make it so. People can think they know the truth when they do not. To be deceived is to believe a thing is true when it is not. The words of Jesus show the problem with the Jews was **they did not believe Moses**. Undoubtedly, they were convinced they *did* believe Moses. Yet, scripture proved they had deceived themselves (because their belief was not consistent with the word of God).

In the passage in question, Jesus went on to say they could not believe his words because they did not believe the words of scripture: "But if ye believe not his writings, how shall ye believe my words?" (Fourth gospel 5:47) Here we see showing respect for all of God's word is critical. When people ignore God's word in one area, the problem is not limited to one issue.

"A little leaven leaveneth the whole lump" (1 Cor 5:6, Gal 5:9). We find this principle stated twice in scripture, but the lesson it teaches is seen in many other passages, including James 2:10-11. The moment someone disregards what scripture says on *one* topic, then they have given themselves permission to do so on any topic. Thereafter, they are not under the authority of God's word; they have put themselves over it (because any authority scripture has comes from them, since they decide when it matters and when it can be ignored).

Leaven has a permeating effect on dough. This pictures what occurs whenever a person takes a pick and choose approach to scripture on any issue. If we are not consistent in our respect for God's word, then our method of assessing truth will produce inconsistent results.

<u>An Ongoing Effect</u>

Jesus' statement, "had ye believed Moses, ye would have believed me: for he wrote of me" (Fourth gospel 5:46) highlights a truth we need to ponder. The Jews' failure to believe Jesus was rooted in their failure to believe Moses and this indicates disregarding scripture in one area has an ongoing detrimental effect.

When we fail to respect God's word in one area, we show disrespect for God, who is the authority behind it all. Believing or not believing the words of Moses has an effect which is not limited to only that part of scripture, as Jesus noted when he went on to say, "But <u>if ye believe not his writings, how shall ye believe my words?</u>" (Fourth gospel 5:47). This principle also applies to other prophets besides Moses, as we see in this verse: "If they hear not Moses **and the prophets**, neither will they be persuaded, though one rose from the dead." (Lk 16:31).

In addition, in this statement Jesus let us know the word of God is the standard by which people will be judged:

> "He that rejecteth me, and receiveth not my words, hath one that judgeth him: the word that I have spoken, the same shall judge him in the last day. For I have not spoken of myself; but the Father which sent me, he gave me a commandment, what I should say, and what I should speak." (Fourth gospel 12:48-49).

What did the words of Moses and the prophets have in common with the words of Jesus? The authority of God was the unifying factor.

Those who do not believe the word of God that came via Moses or the prophets, will not believe Jesus' words, for the source of the words (God) is the same in both cases. This is why those who love the truth must exercise a **consistent** respect for the authority of scripture.

The following words were written to Timothy, but they also offer good counsel to every believer: "Study to shew thyself approved unto God, a workman that needeth not to be ashamed, rightly dividing the word of truth" (2 Tm 2:15). [The word "study" translates a Greek word that is more often translated as "be diligent," "give diligence," and "do thy diligence" (cf. 2 Tm 4:9 & 21, Titus 3:12, 2 Pt 1:10, 3:14). Therefore, the Greek lets us know "rightly dividing the word of truth" involves a diligence that goes beyond the idea of 'study' which is promoted today.]

How can a person confirm they have rightly divided the word of truth? A formal education cannot guarantee a person will not be deceived. "The chief priests and the scribes and the chief of the people sought to destroy" Jesus (Lk 19:47). "The Pharisees and lawyers rejected the counsel of God against themselves" (Lk 7:30). Jesus told his disciples to beware of "the doctrine of the Pharisees and of the Sadducees" (Mt 16:12), so this proves being counted among the educated elite is not the same as being "approved unto God."

<u>Saul of Tarsus, Be Ashamed</u>

Jesus warned his disciples, "the time cometh, that whosoever killeth you will think that he doeth God service" (Fourth gospel 16:2). Jesus was talking about men like Saul of Tarsus.

Saul was a member of the educated elite, "a Hebrew of the Hebrews; as touching the law, a Pharisee" (Phl 3:5), but he was not taught the truth of God's word. He learned to think like his teachers (a method of discerning between truth and error which is fundamentally flawed).

We can learn a lot about how to "be not deceived" by considering Saul of Tarsus before he received his wake-up call on the road to Damascus. No doubt Saul *thought* he knew God's word, but he was using a wrong measure of truth.

When people use their current beliefs as their measure of truth, it will not help them see when they are in error. Saul likely felt very assured because he agreed with highly regarded religious scholars. Yet, this false measure could only help to keep him in bondage to deception.

At that time Saul was in ignorance. He himself later said he had been "a blasphemer, and a persecutor, and injurious: but I obtained mercy, because I did *it* ignorantly in unbelief" (1 Tm 1:13). Surely, he could have recited the words of scripture. So, what can explain his ignorance at that point? Did the words of scripture confuse Saul and cause him to be in ignorance and unbelief? Or was he blind to the truth in scripture because he put confidence in man and learned the teachings of men which make void the word of God?

Saul of Tarsus had not been "rightly dividing the word of truth" prior to his encounter with Jesus on the Damascus road. He was wrongly dividing God's word. He needed "to be ashamed" of his false beliefs and of the method of assessing truth which led him to think he was doing good when he was doing just the opposite. Yet, after he learned the truth on the Damascus road, Saul did not dig in his heels and continue to resist the truth (as was the case with the religious leaders who knew Jesus had risen from the dead and still would not repent).

Deception Inside of the Church

Those in the church can also be deceived and the verses warning believers to "be not deceived" (cf. Lk 21:8, 1 Cor 6:9, 15:33, Gal 6:7) along with other passages make this clear. The opening words of Galatians 3, "O foolish Galatians, who hath bewitched you, that ye should not obey the truth" is just one of the many places where the writers of the New Testament dealt with errors among believers.

In our day, the tolerance of error is fostered when people value unity above truth and those who contend for truth are said to be 'divisive'. Tolerating falsehood was a problem that brought a strong rebuke to the church in Corinth. They tolerated those who held contrary ideas on the resurrection, which earned the church this reprimand: "If Christ be preached that he rose from the dead, how say some among you that there is no resurrection of the dead?" (1 Cor 15:12) Contrary ideas cannot both be true, so when believers agree to tolerate falsehood, they are not fostering a love of the truth [more on this later].

When the people in Elijah's day worshiped both the LORD and Baal, he did not call for tolerance. Rather, he offered this rebuke: "How long halt ye between two opinions? if the LORD be God, follow him: but if Baal, *then* follow him" (1 Kgs 18:21). Keep in mind Elijah's rebuke of those who were "between two opinions" as we consider a rebuke to the church from Jesus himself.

The words, "He that hath an ear, let him hear what the Spirit saith unto the churches" show up seven times in the Book of Revelation (Rv 2:7, 11, 17 & 29, 3:6, 13 & 22), so followers of Jesus should ponder what was said to the churches. For now, though, notice what Jesus said to "the angel of the church of the Laodiceans" (Rv 3:14):

> "thou sayest, I am rich, and increased with goods, and have need of nothing; and knowest not that thou art wretched, and miserable, and poor, and blind, and naked" (Rv 3:17).

If people think they are "rich" and "have need of nothing" when their actual condition is "poor, and blind, and naked," clearly their beliefs are not a model for others to follow. Jesus' rebuke was not directed to pagans or unbelievers; it was to the church! This should act as a shot across the bow to warn us not to assume our view, our church's view, or beliefs in the so-called 'early church' are necessarily correct.

<u>Escaping the Bonds of Deception</u>

As was noted earlier, the words "ye shall know the truth, and the truth shall make you free" (Fourth gospel 8:32) were directed to people who "believed on" Jesus and would "continue in" his word (Fourth gospel 8:31). So a consistent respect for God's word is set forth as a condition for those who want to "know the truth" and be set free by it. Since "the fear of the LORD *is* **the beginning of knowledge**" (Prv 1:7), "the fear of the LORD" must be the foundation of our efforts to find the truth.

Jesus rebuked the scholars of his day for "making the word of God of none effect through your tradition" (Mk 7:13), and their failure to show a consistent respect for God's word was at the root of the problem. Those men passed along their beliefs, instead of bearing witness to God's word and upholding it as the standard of truth.

Encouraging people to trust the teachings of men goes against the counsel of God's word. Thus, <u>it is a telltale sign when one has to cite the teachings of men in order to make their case.</u>

Those who have let the teachings of men serve as the foundation for their beliefs may think the statement, "in the multitude of counsellors there is safety" (Prv 11:14, 24:6) defends the practice of looking to the opinions of men when one wants to learn the truth on biblical issues. Yet those words cannot possibly be encouraging people to think they can avoid being deceived by believing ideas which are espoused by a large quantity of people.

If people trusted the multitude of religious experts and educated men to tell them what to make of Jesus, would that have helped them to discover the truth about Jesus? No. Rather, the teachings of those men prejudiced people against Jesus and caused many to be blind to the truth. Popularity is not a proper measure of truth. So those who think the quantity of people who hold a belief *is* a good indicator of whether or not that idea is true are using a false balance. Moreover, a multitude of common, everyday people can also be wrong.

When Jesus asked his disciples to tell him who people said he was, they told him, "John the Baptist; but some *say*, Elias; and others *say*, that one of the old prophets is risen again" (Lk 9:19). When people hold opposing views on a matter, would their counsel offer "safety" if they constituted a multitude? At one point in Paul's ministry "the multitude of the people followed after, crying, Away with him." But their unity and their number did not mean their words were wise. Also, we read in Exodus 23:2, "Thou shalt not follow a multitude to *do* evil." So, one cannot say going along with the crowd is encouraged by scripture.

Safety in Numbers?

Groupthink and the wisdom of this world tells people *'there is safety in numbers.'* Being aligned with a large number of people can provide a degree of security in some situations. It is a fallacy, however, to take this as a universal principle. Still, because of this kind of thinking, many do assume following a multitude of people is the best way to avoid error on intellectual issues even though scripture indicates this is not a wise practice.

Verses have already been cited in this regard, but consider two other passages. Acts 14:4 says, "the multitude of the city was divided: and part held with the Jews, and part with the apostles." Another passage also reports a dispute which occurred among some people who were listening to Jesus teach: "There was much murmuring among the people concerning him: for some said, He is a good man: others said, Nay; but he deceiveth the people" (Fourth gospel 7:12). Would those who stood with the majority in those disputes be more likely to be correct?

If we think the number of people who hold a belief is an indication of whether or not the belief is true, then we are using a wrong standard. If a multitude of people believe something, all it does is prove those people *think* the idea is true. There are large groups of people who believe false ideas, so their numbers cannot mean those beliefs are worthy of consideration.

If people believe something, that does not make it true. If they reject an idea, that does not make it false. Acceptance by a person or group is not what makes something true. Citing the number of people who say 'x' is true in order to convince others to believe the idea, is not a God-honoring way to make an argument.

When we make a case on a biblical issue using a measure of truth which is not compatible with the counsel found in scripture, then we are asking others to rely on a false measure. People are taught to rely on an unbiblical method when they are led to believe an idea is likely true if a large number of people believe it. The majority is not always wrong, but they are not always right either.

<u>It Gets Better with Age?</u>

When people are deciding whether something is true or worthy of consideration, another factor they often look to is time. If an idea *'has been around for a long time'* or it *'was written about long ago'* this tends to make it more credible in the eyes of men. The question is: Does the length of time since an idea was first advanced hold up as a reliable indicator of whether or not an idea is true? No. Consider two examples that show this to be the case.

Example #1: there were reports written almost a hundred years ago which promoted *'Dawson's dawn man'* as a great scientific find and cited it as proof of monkey-to-man evolution. This idea was believed in the past, so does this make it credible? Because it was promoted in respected publications and peer-reviewed literature, does this give it more credibility? What if a majority of scholars accepted this idea? What would all of this prove?

Neither time, nor agreement among men, nor acceptance by experts are reliable measures for assessing truth. So, even if a person has all of those things, they would still be using a false method if they based their judgment on those things. It turns out *'Dawson's dawn man'* (aka *'Piltdown man'*) was, decades later, exposed as a fraud. But what of the writings of men in all the peer-reviewed literature and textbooks which promoted this as truth? All those experts and all their writings worked to deceive everyone who relied on them!

Some will say a *'time-tested'* idea happens only over a longer period. However, the beliefs of men who lived long ago might be false, since men who lived in the past could make mistakes and/or be deceived, so knowing *when* a statement was made (or the fact that a belief was held by people who lived long ago) does not tell us if it is true or not. Moreover, the passage of time will never make a false statement true because, unlike wine, error does not improve with age.

Example #2: for over 2000 years most Jews have believed Jesus was not the Messiah, which is why they do not follow him. But even though a large group of people has accepted this idea for a very long time, they are still deceived nonetheless.

Tradition?

Does scripture indicate ideas that are called 'tradition' are more likely to be true? No. Earlier we considered the time when Jesus rebuked the religious experts of his day for "Making the word of God of none effect through your tradition, which ye have delivered" (Mk 7:13). Yet, it is fairly common to hear teachers refer to a belief as 'tradition' when they want to give an idea *an air of authority*. But, teaching people to put confidence in the traditions of men is not a biblical method.

Read what Jesus said about the traditions of men in Matthew 15:1-9 and Mark 7:1-13. Colossians 2:8 offered this caution to the brethren of that day, "Beware lest any man spoil you through philosophy and vain deceit, after the tradition of men, after the rudiments of the world, and not after Christ."

Some things that honor God are called tradition, so not all tradition is bad. How can one tell a God-honoring tradition from a tradition which makes the word of God of no effect? Test it!

The source of a tradition is what makes the difference, as we can see from verses like this: "Now we command you, brethren, in the name of our Lord Jesus Christ, that ye withdraw yourselves from every brother that walketh disorderly, and not after the tradition which he **received of us**" (2 Th 3:6). Here again, we need to consider the source. A tradition taught by the God-inspired writers of scripture would have God's authority, while a tradition of men is simply that.

When the traditions of men are promoted, people end up trusting in the authority of men. This leads to the teachings of men being cited as the measure of truth and makes the word of God "of none effect."

<u>Reliable Sources?</u>

Many people look at a person's credentials when they are trying to decide what to believe. The problem with this is people will often drop their guard because they put confidence in someone's credentials. For example, those who think group 'x' promotes the truth will tend to adopt ideas that are taught by people who are affiliated with the group and/or by teachers who have been trained at an institution with ties to the group. Yet, those things provide no guarantee of truth.

Man-made institutions will grant degrees, bestow honors, and endow people with authority. When men honor other men, what does that tell us? Where a knowledge of physical laws or an application of them in a particular field is concerned, men issue credentials to others who learn the skills needed to be proficient in a given field. This helps to keep the public safe. In the case of pilots, electricians, architects, etc. this system yields results that are fairly consistent and usually reliable. But, is it a good idea where God's word is concerned?

We expect no one will be granted a pilot's license unless they have learned what it takes to deliver the results which every pilot should be able to deliver (a safe flight from takeoff to landing). When it comes to God's word, do the credentials which are issued by men insure a similar degree of accuracy will be seen in the results? No. When men are asked what the Bible teaches on a given issue, some men who have been ordained or have PhDs will say 'x' is true and some of them will say 'x' is not true.

This same problem shows up in scripture when the teachings of men were used as the basis of a religious education. The Sadducees and the Pharisees were two of the leading religious groups of Jesus' day, and those two groups held contradictory views because they used different measures to determine what was true. Acts 23:8 tells us, "the Sadducees say that there is no resurrection, neither angel, nor spirit: but the Pharisees confess both." They contradicted each other; so while both groups could be wrong, they could not both be right.

<u>Were Pharisees Better than Sadducees?</u>

Acts 23:8 lets us know large groups and powerful men can espouse beliefs that are not true. Therefore, it is never safe for one to assume a teaching is true simply because the teaching is believed by people who have been formally trained in religious matters. Worse yet, it is not safe to assume those who teach the truth on some issues will necessarily teach the truth on other issues. Those who assumed the Pharisees taught the truth because they affirmed the "resurrection"

were wrong. Both groups undermined the authority of God's word. The Sadducees and Pharisees were not the only groups Jesus spoke out against, but he specifically warned his disciples about something these groups had in common and his point can still teach us today.

Jesus told his disciples, "Take heed and beware of the leaven of the Pharisees and of the Sadducees" (Mt 16:6). After he had explained his words to them it says, "Then understood they how that he bade them not beware of the leaven of bread, but of the doctrine of the Pharisees and of the Sadducees" (Mt 16:12). Jesus used the picture of "leaven" to portray their "doctrine," and it applied to both groups. So what can we learn from his one warning regarding two very different groups?

Jesus spoke of "the doctrine of the Pharisees and of the Sadducees" as if it was something they had in common, and this points us to a trait or practice common to both groups. His warning was not against their teaching on particular issues, since they were not in agreement on many matters. Where do we see the unity in the doctrine of these two groups? It is found in the teachings of men – not in their views on various issues, but in *their practice of promoting the teachings of men in addition to God's word*, for both groups did this.

Keep in mind, "leaven" is something that has a permeating influence. This is why it is a perfect word picture for the practice of promoting the teachings of men. Scripture has authority because it is "of God" and this authority is usurped when the teachings of men are cited as an additional source of truth on biblical issues.

Practices which Undermine God's Authority

Both the Sadducees and Pharisees thought they were right and each group produced clones who were taught to trust in the teachings that were promoted by their group. Elsewhere, Jesus said the "Pharisees and scribes" were "making the word of God of none effect" through their tradition (Mk 7:13), so the teachings which are promoted by men and religious groups can actually counteract the effect of God's word.

As has been noted, Psalm 118:8 says, "*It is* better to trust in the LORD than to put confidence in man." Those who think there is an exception to this verse so long as they only put their confidence in men who are highly respected should note the very next verse: "*It is* better to trust in the LORD than to put confidence in princes" (Ps 118:9).

Had people merely put confidence in the wrong group? No. While the Pharisees and the Sadducees differed on some of their beliefs, both groups undermined God's word by promoting the traditions of men.

"A little leaven leaveneth the whole lump" (Gal 5:9) and this is why even a little of the "leaven of the Pharisees and of the Sadducees" made the word of God of no effect to those who trusted in them.

<u>Good Counsel? By What Standard?</u>

When we seek the counsel of others, how can we tell if the counsel we get is good counsel? In 1 Kings 12 we see how one man made this decision. When Rehoboam took over as king, the people asked him to lighten the burden imposed on them by his father. At that point, he sought counsel as to how he should answer the people.

"And king Rehoboam consulted with the old men, that stood before Solomon his father while he yet lived, and said, How do ye advise that I may answer this people?" (1 Kgs 12:6). They advised him to lessen the burden, "but he forsook the counsel of the old men, which they had given him, and consulted with the young men" (1 Kgs 12:8).

The advice of the young men was just the opposite. They told him to greatly increase the burdens on the people. What did Rehoboam do?

"The king answered the people roughly, and forsook the old men's counsel that they gave him; And spake to them after the counsel of the young men" (1 Kgs 12:13-14).

The king got contrary advice from two groups, therefore, the counsel of both groups could not be good. Rehoboam did what men often do, he chose to listen to those men *who told him what he wanted to hear.* (Notice 1 Kgs 12:8 first says, "he forsook the counsel of the old men," and only after that does it tell us he "consulted with the young men.")

Choosing the counsel that suits us is a lot like a practice Paul warned about in 2 Timothy. He described people who "will not endure sound doctrine" but who prefer teachers who say what they want to hear – "after their own lusts shall they heap to themselves teachers, having itching ears" (2 Tm 4:3). If we seek good counsel, then our preference cannot be our standard of measure.

<u>A Multitude of God's Counsel?</u>

We find another instructive passage on seeking counsel in Joshua 9. The inhabitants of Gibeon crafted a cover story and made it look as if they had come from a far country in order to deceive the children of Israel into making a deal with them:

"They did work wilily, and went and made as if they had been ambassadors, and took old sacks upon their asses, and wine bottles, old, and rent, and bound up; And old shoes and clouted upon their feet, and old garments upon them; and all the bread of their provision was dry and moldy." (Jos 9:4-5).

It worked. "And Joshua made peace with them, and made a league with them, to let them live: and the princes of the congregation swore unto them" (Jos 9:15). They were deceived because they chose to lean on their own understanding instead of seeking the LORD's counsel. "And the men took of their victuals, and asked not *counsel* at the mouth of the LORD" (Jos 9:14).

If someone who was as in touch with the LORD as Joshua can make the mistake of failing to check with the LORD because he trusted in his own ability to make a reasonable inference, then we need to learn from his mistake! When it comes to issues in scripture, since we know men can *think* they are promoting God's truth when they are not, the wisest thing to do is to seek the counsel of the LORD on every issue.

Seeking counsel is encouraged in verses like, "Where no counsel is, the people fall: but in the multitude of counsellors there is safety" (Prv 11:14) and "Without counsel purposes are disappointed: but in the multitude of counsellors they are established" (Prv 15:22). Yet a verse like, "For by wise counsel thou shalt make thy war" (Prv 24:6) shows us all counsel is not the same. So, how can people know if the counsel they get is "wise" or not?

In speaking to the brethren in Ephesus, Paul said he had not failed to declare to them "all the counsel of God" (Acts 20:27), and this is more than merely advice on a concern we may have at a given moment. Scripture gives us God's counsel, so those who heed the word of God could say what the author of Psalm 16:7 said: "I will bless the LORD, who hath given me counsel."

Bad Unity

"The kings of the earth set themselves, and the rulers take counsel together, against the LORD and against his anointed, *saying*, Let us break their bands asunder, and cast away their cords from us" (Ps 2:2-3).

They "take counsel together" and have a unity of purpose, but surely this was not "wise" counsel. The idea is so ridiculous that it merited this response: "He that sitteth in the heavens shall laugh" (Ps 2:4).

Bad unity and counsel of men that is foolish or evil shows up in many other verses. 1 Kings12:28 says, "the king took counsel, and made two calves of gold." A king of Israel should have known such counsel was not good (even if a multitude of 'experts' advised him to do so). Was better counsel available? Yes, it was.

"Woe to the rebellious children, saith the LORD, that take counsel, but not of me" (Isa 30:1). So taking counsel is not good enough. The source of one's counsel makes all the difference!

When people do not want the LORD's counsel they find a substitute for it, as we see in this verse: "My people ask counsel at their stocks, and their staff declareth unto them" (Hos 4:12). That practice seems to have the same sort of effect as came from following the consensus of the religious leaders in Jesus' day – "The Pharisees and lawyers rejected the counsel of God against themselves" (Lk 7:30). Worse yet, when "the chief priests, and the scribes, and the elders of the people" (Mt 26:3) put their heads together, they "consulted that they might take Jesus by subtlety, and kill *him*" (Mt 26:4).

The Wisdom of This World

This world's wisdom tells us to esteem experts, value their opinion, and heed their advice. Endless honors are bestowed by men (and the organizations they run) upon those who meet their standards. So, is putting confidence in men who are honored by other men a wise thing to do? Does a theology degree or ordination by some religious group make a person less susceptible to deception?

God's word does not encourage people to value the opinions of men. Scripture takes a dim view of the world's measure of wisdom and the honors bestowed by men:

- "hath not God made foolish the wisdom of this world?" (1 Cor 1:20);
- "in the wisdom of God the world by wisdom knew not God" (1 Cor 1:21);
- "not many wise men after the flesh, not many mighty, not many noble, *are called*" (1 Cor 1:26);
- "the wisdom of this world is foolishness with God. For it is written, He taketh the wise in their own craftiness. And again, The Lord knoweth the thoughts of the wise, that they are vain. Therefore let no man glory in men" (1 Cor 3:19-21);

- **"How can ye believe**, which receive honor one of another, and seek not the honor that *cometh* from God only?" (Fourth gospel 5:44).

Honor? From What Source?

Jesus linked belief to honor when he contrasted the two sources of honor: "How can ye believe, which receive honor one of another, and seek not the honor that *cometh* from God only?" (Fourth gospel 5:44). Jesus put those two sources of honor in opposition to each other. [Note: the word "can" refers to ability, so men who "receive honor one of another" instead of seeking "the honor that *cometh* from God only" may be jeopardizing their own ability to "believe."]

Seeking the honor that comes "from God only" would be in line with the choice Moses made (cf. Heb 11:26), and in line with the requirement that those who come to God must believe God "is a rewarder of them that diligently seek him" (Heb 11:6).

Scripture also says, "before honor *is* humility" (Prv 15:33, 18:12) and this parallels what we read in James 4:10 "Humble yourselves in the sight of the Lord, and he shall lift you up." Those words were written to the "brethren" (Jas 3:1). James contrasted the very different results of pride and humility when he gave this bit of counsel:

"God resisteth the proud, but giveth grace unto the humble. Submit yourselves therefore to God" (Jas 4:6-7).

Peter made the same point when he wrote to "the strangers" (1 Pt 1:1) who were "elect" (1 Pt 1:2) and said:

"all of you be subject one to another, and be clothed with humility: for God resisteth the proud, and giveth grace to the humble. Humble yourselves therefore under the mighty hand of God" (1 Pt 5:5-6).

This tells us how we respond to God's word makes all the difference (cf. 1 Th 2:13).

Since James also told the brethren, "draw nigh to God, and he will draw nigh to you" (Jas 4:8), believers who say they want to be closer to God need to begin moving in that direction. One way believers can do this is to "let this mind be in you, which was also in Christ Jesus" (Phl 2:5). Jesus himself expressed this mind in these words: "as I hear, I judge: and my judgment is just; because I seek not mine own will, but the will of the Father which hath sent me" (Fourth gospel 5:30).

Instead of seeking his own will, Jesus sought the will of the Father and he said that meant his judgment was just: "my judgment is just; because I seek not mine own will, but the will of the Father." Thus, if we want our judgment to be just, we should let this mind be in us.

Reality Check

Also, notice what Jesus said after he spoke about honor from God:

"How can ye believe, which receive honor one of another, and seek not the honor that *cometh* from God only? Do not think that I will accuse you to the Father: **there is one that accuseth you**, *even* **Moses, in whom ye trust**. For had ye believed Moses, ye would have believed me: for he wrote of me. But if ye believe not his writings, how shall ye believe my words?" (Fourth gospel 5:44-47).

The Moses they trusted in was their accuser! How? The writings of Moses were preserved in scripture and his words showed they were dishonoring Moses and God, for they had not believed Moses' words. [Notice this shows how people can convince themselves they trust in the truths of scripture, even when words that are written in scripture testify against them. The same thing occurs when those who say they believe in Jesus hold beliefs that are contrary to the testimony of any of the God-inspired writers of scripture].

Their beliefs were based on the teachings of men. *By that standard they judged themselves to be Moses' followers.* However, they used a wrong measure, and false measures lead people to flawed results. When people judge based on a false standard they will be deceived, for they will assume their beliefs are correct, although they are not.

God preserved the writings of Moses in scripture and Moses' words accused them because his words proved they did not believe what he said. But they did not need Jesus to tell them they were deceived because scripture already did that.

When the "had ye believed Moses..." verse was considered above, we learned how it teaches the need to be consistent in our regard for all of scripture. Sadly, reading the Old Testament is avoided by many who claim to love Jesus. Yet he said, Moses wrote of him! So we can learn of him by reading what Moses wrote. Moreover, Jesus also said, "But if ye believe not his writings, how shall ye believe my words?" (Fourth gospel 5:47), for the authority of God was the same in both cases.

"According to the Scriptures"

In 1 Corinthians 15:1, Paul explicitly refers to "the gospel" and says:

> "Christ died for our sins **according to the scriptures**; And that he was buried, and that he rose again the third day **according to the scriptures**" (1 Cor 15:3-4).

Twice he said, "according to the scriptures," so "the gospel" rests on the authority of the Old Testament.

Moreover, the phrase "it is written" appears in the Bible over and over, as Jesus and later the apostles cited the authority of God's word in regard to whatever matter they were dealing with at the time. If Jesus and the apostles linked their teachings to the words in scripture, then we need to be paying attention to the Old Testament.

Also, in Acts 26:22-23, Paul spoke the following words before Agrippa and indicated everything he taught about Jesus was already noted in the Old Testament:

> "I continue unto this day, witnessing both to small and great, **saying none other things than those which the prophets and Moses did say should come**: That Christ should suffer, *and* that he should be the first that should rise from the dead, and should shew light unto the people, and to the Gentiles."

Those who believed in *a Moses* who was not the Moses of scripture should have known better, since the measure of God's word warned them against trusting in "lying words." Jeremiah had warned those of Judah who sought to worship the LORD, "trust ye not in lying words" (Jer 7:4) and "Behold, ye trust in lying words, that cannot profit" (Jer 7:8). Those words were spoken to people who had been deceived by the teachings of men. Therefore, we ought to consider the remedy he prescribed: "Thus saith the LORD of hosts, the God of Israel, Amend your ways and your doings" (Jer 7:3).

Learn from Other People's Mistakes

Jeremiah had much to say on the topic of false assertions being attributed to the LORD and about people choosing the words of men over the word of God. Jeremiah 2:8 shows one should not assume it is safe to trust the men who are part of the religious establishment: "They that handle the law knew me not: the pastors also transgressed against me, and the prophets prophesied by Baal, and walked after *things that* do not profit." Other passages offer similar descriptions:

- "from the prophet even unto the priest every one dealeth falsely" (Jer 8:10);
- "Many pastors have destroyed my vineyard" (Jer 12:10);
- "the LORD said unto me, The prophets prophesy lies in my name: I sent them not, neither have I commanded them, neither spake unto them: they prophesy unto you a false vision and divination, and a thing of naught, and the deceit of their heart" (Jer 14:14);
- "Woe be unto the pastors that destroy and scatter the sheep of my pasture! saith the LORD" (Jer 23:1);
- "Thus saith the LORD of hosts, Hearken not unto the words of the prophets that prophesy unto you: they make you vain: they speak a vision of their own heart, and not out of the mouth of the LORD" (Jer 23:16).

If the words of men are assumed to be true, it can keep people from the truth in God's word that can turn them around, as in this passage:

"I have not sent these prophets, yet they ran: I have not spoken to them, yet they prophesied. But **if they had stood in my counsel, and had caused my people to hear my words**, then they should have turned them from their evil way, and from the evil of their doings" (Jer 23:21-22).

If they had stood in the LORD's counsel and caused his people to hear his words, then those teachers could have made a difference!

The LORD went on to say, "<u>he that hath my word, let him speak my word faithfully</u>" (Jer 23:28). Obedience to this principle put Jeremiah on a collision course with the religious establishment of his day because he spoke the word of the LORD "faithfully" (which showed they had *not* done so).

Those who attributed the ideas of men to the LORD were actually guilty of stealing the word of the LORD:

"I *am* against the prophets, saith the LORD, that **steal my words** every one from his neighbor. Behold, I *am* against the prophets, saith the LORD, that use their tongues, and say, He saith. Behold, I *am* against them that prophesy false dreams, saith the LORD, and do tell them, and cause my people to err by their lies, and by their lightness" (Jer 23:30-32).

If we consider the whole context, then it becomes clear that not being faithful to the word of the LORD was equated to stealing it.

Choosing Falsehood over Truth?

The pastors, prophets, and priests of that day were not the only ones at fault. According to the LORD, the people wanted to hear falsehood: "The prophets prophesy falsely, and the priests bear rule by their means; and my people love to have it so" (Jer 5:31). The LORD also put it this way, "my people have committed two evils; they have forsaken me the fountain of living waters, *and* hewed them out cisterns, broken cisterns, that can hold no water" (Jer 2:13). [In scripture, terms like "the washing of water by the word" (Eph 5:26) show how water was used as a picture of God's word – and when people forsake the LORD ("the fountain of living waters"), they reject the truth provided by the word of the LORD and turn to a self-made system that does not hold water.]

Jeremiah was talking about a people who had a form of religion, yet they did not want the LORD's word, as the LORD noted when he said:

"To whom shall I speak, and give warning, that they may hear? behold, their ear is uncircumcised, and they cannot hearken: behold, **the word of the LORD is unto them a reproach**; they have no delight in it" (Jer 6:10).

Changing their beliefs on particular issues would not fix the problem. The LORD, speaking through Jeremiah said, "Amend **your ways and your doings**." (Jer 7:3 & 5, 26:13). They needed to change their methods and their behavior, because beliefs do not occur in a vacuum. People always use some process to decide what they will believe, and if they have believed false ideas, then they have relied on a flawed process, flawed data, or both. In any case, it is surely worse when a person turns away from the truth because it is something they want to avoid.

Why would a person not want to know the truth? No one likes to feel shame or embarrassment. If something leads us to feel awkward or embarrassed, we do our best to avoid it. So those who put confidence in the opinions of men will tend to resist whenever facts arise that call their view into question, and this is not limited to the realm of religion, as the following example shows.

In the 1800s a man cited evidence that proved if surgeons washed their hands between patients it would save lives. However, those who trusted in *'established scientific and medical opinions'* took offense, for this would mean they were wrong to trust all the experts who said hand washing was pointless. They would have to admit their methods had resulted in harm. So they suppressed the truth, ridiculed the man and, thus, avoided embarrassment.

Many years (and deaths) later, further proof finally meant the truth could no longer be suppressed and, at that point, hand washing was adopted as standard practice.

<u>Embarrassed by the Truth?</u>

Scripture presents the standard of truth and beliefs can be tested by this measure to see if they line up with scripture. "The word of God *is* quick, and powerful" (Heb 4:12) and, if it is faithfully communicated, it can turn people away from errant beliefs and practices (cf. Jer 23:22).

What makes the difference when biblical correction is offered is how we react to it. When the truth shows we have been misled, are we thankful for it or embarrassed by it? Remember, the fear of men (i.e., their opinions and perhaps their ridicule) is something we must avoid:

"The fear of man bringeth a snare: but whoso putteth his trust in the LORD shall be safe" (Prv 29:25).

We will not be embarrassed by any truth presented by scripture if we love the truth. When Jesus said, "I am the way, the truth, and the life" (Fourth gospel 14:6) he identified himself with truth. So the way we treat the truth is an indication of how we would treat Jesus!

Still, some reject the love of the truth and we can see how dangerous this is in what 2 Thessalonians 2:10 says about "them that perish" – "they received not the love of the truth, that they might be saved."

<u>Holding Contrary Views</u>

Delay is one way people avoid biblical correction, and that seems to be one of the responses to Paul's talk on Mars' hill:

"And when they heard of the resurrection of the dead, some mocked: and others said, We will hear thee again of this *matter.* So Paul departed from among them. Howbeit certain men clave unto him, and believed" (Acts 17:32-34).

Scripture lets us know putting the truth on hold can be a risky thing to do, and on that day "some mocked," some "believed," and others put off a decision until later. Another way people deal with truth when it is contrary to their current beliefs is they put truth on par with error by acting as if it is okay to believe ideas which are contrary to one another, much like the people did in 1 Kings 18.

In 1 Kings 18:21 Elijah the prophet rebuked the practice of holding contrary views: "Elijah came unto all the people, and said, How long halt ye **between two opinions**? if the LORD *be* God, follow him: but if Baal, *then* follow him."

Amazingly, Elijah challenged them to "follow" Baal *if Baal is God*, so their divided loyalty meant they were not even following Baal.

His most critical barb was not against Baal worship. Rather, it was against their willingness to live in the space "between two opinions" (and act as if the truth does not need to be respected).

Elijah's premise is obvious. The LORD and Baal cannot both be God. So it is foolish to follow them both. The claims are mutually exclusive. If one is true, the other must be false. Nevertheless, the people were acting as if both could be true, and in doing so, they were tolerating obvious falsehood.

Acting as if contrary ideas are both true destroys respect for the truth! In order to accommodate the worship of other gods, scripture has to be set aside. However, the idea that people *can* worship other gods *and* believe God's word is not a problem for those who tell themselves it is okay to believe and/or tolerate contrary ideas.

It is unreasonable to worship the LORD and Baal because they cannot both be God.

Jesus said, "Thou shalt worship the Lord thy God, and him only shalt thou serve" (Mt 4:10, Lk 4:8). Therefore, those who serve other gods cannot worship the LORD **according to the scriptures**.

<u>'Agree to Disagree?'</u>

Today many churchgoers will say, *'we will have to agree to disagree'* when they want to cut-off a debate over some Bible issue. This is not the same as when a person is seeking to learn the truth on an issue and they hear someone state a conclusion on the issue that may be contrary to scripture. When someone is seeking the truth on an issue, the fact that God's word has yet to show them the truth on that issue is something they want to remedy. Those in this condition who may walk away from a discussion are not 'agreeing to disagree,' for they have not yet been convinced they know the truth on the issue.

On the other hand, if people who claim to know the truth on an issue hold contrary views on that issue, they cannot both be right because contrary ideas cannot both be true. In this situation, if one of those parties says, 'we will just have to agree to disagree' in order to cut-off discussion of that issue, is that person seeking the truth? No. But it is a way to avoid having one's view subjected to the test of scripture. 'Agree to disagree' is an empty phrase that is meant to sound virtuous even as it is being used to set aside the question of truth. While this keeps up the appearance of unity, it does so at the expense of truth.

In effect, those in Elijah's day who worshipped the LORD and Baal had adopted the 'agree to disagree' model in their own minds. It does not make holding contrary ideas right or logical, but it does avoid having to choose between one belief and the other.

A 'spirit of unity' is a primary goal for some church groups in our day. This can lead members of the group to resist the truth when it calls into question some belief or practice which is promoted by the group. While promoting a 'spirit of unity' may sound like a good idea, it is not a biblical idea. It is wrong because it makes unity the goal.

Instead, we should be "endeavoring to keep the unity **of the Spirit**" (Eph 4:3), and we dare not switch the order of those words!

"The unity of the Spirit" is not the same as 'a spirit of unity.'

'A spirit of unity' might exist at a ball game or a Baal worship meeting. "The unity of the Spirit," however, has truth as a built-in condition – because "the Spirit" is "the Spirit **of truth**". So we need to evaluate the basis of the "unity" that is being promoted or sought.

<u>"The Spirit of Truth"</u>

Jesus talked about "the Spirit of truth" (Fourth gospel 14:17, 15:26, 16:13) and told his disciples, "when he, the Spirit of truth, is come, he will guide you into all truth" (Fourth gospel 16:13). Scripture also tells believers about "salvation through sanctification of the Spirit and belief of the truth" (2 Th 2:13). Passages such as those teach us "the Spirit" and truth go hand in hand. Therefore, a unity established apart from truth <u>cannot be</u> "the unity **of** the Spirit."

Moreover, the truth causes division! It distinguishes itself from error, and it calls our judgment into question when we have believed ideas that cannot stand up to the light of truth. As has already been noted, Jesus identified himself with the truth. Yet, he also told of the division he would bring: "Suppose ye that I am come to give peace on earth? I tell you, Nay; but rather division" (Lk 12:51). So if truth causes division, how is "the unity of the Spirit" even possible?

It is possible because the truth divides those who do not have or want the truth from those who do – while, at the same time, the truth unites those who have a love of the truth. Where we end up depends on us.

Psalm 86:11 says, "Teach me thy way, O LORD; I will walk in thy truth: unite my heart to fear thy name." This suggests a heart committed to a respect for the authority of God is linked to:

(A) being taught by God, and
(B) a willingness to heed his word and conform our walk to it.

In the passages where believers (i.e., the brethren) were said to be of "one accord," their unity was not achieved by downplaying truth. It was the result of them being taught by "the Spirit of truth." [The term "one accord" does not by itself imply a love of the truth, for it was also used of those who unified against the truth, such as when "the Jews made insurrection with one accord against Paul" (Acts 18:12).]

What was the focal point for the unity among the brethren? It was their willingness to follow Jesus in submitting to the authority of God. This is what Jesus indicated he had done when he made statements such as:

- "I do nothing of myself; but as my Father hath taught me, I speak these things" (Fourth gospel 8:28);
- "I have not spoken of myself; but the Father which sent me, he gave me a commandment, what I should say, and what I should speak" (Fourth gospel 12:49).

Truth or Opinion?

Jesus once said, "No man can serve two masters: for either he will hate the one, and love the other; or else he will hold to the one, and despise the other" (Mt 6:24), and this principle needs to shape how we see things. For example, when the people of Elijah's day worshiped the LORD and Baal, were they serving two masters? No, they were despising the LORD **by** worshipping Baal. Even if they told themselves they *were* serving the LORD *and* Baal, their belief did not make it so, for "No man can serve two masters."

Similarly, one does not serve the cause of truth by holding on to error. Still, some will try to suppress the discussion of biblical evidence that is contrary to their view on an issue, and saying it *'causes division'* is one of the ways this is done. But, when this or other excuses are used to dodge the issue of authority, the truth is sacrificed in the process.

The process of distinguishing truth from error is too often clouded by faulty reasoning. For example, there is a difference between disputes over what color to paint a wall or the volume of the worship music, and a debate over what is true on some biblical issue. The difference should be obvious, but it is sometimes ignored.

When people cannot justify their belief on some biblical issue, they naturally want to avoid discussions that would require them to do so. Some will do this by acting as if the issue that is being discussed is a matter of personal preference, because the standard in such matters is one's opinion, not truth.

Whenever someone acts as if what scripture says on a biblical issue can be treated as a matter of preference, please remind that person that what is written in scripture is not a matter of personal preference, it is a matter of truth. Some issues do involve a matter of conscience, but scripture tells us what those are; it is not for us to pick and choose.

<u>Heeding Jesus Regarding New Things</u>

In seeking to discern the truth on biblical issues, we must consider the idea of compatibility. If we join two things that are not compatible, the result will not be good, and Jesus taught this idea in these words:

> "no man putteth new wine into old bottles; else the new wine will burst the bottles, and be spilled, and the bottles shall perish. But new wine must be put into new bottles; and both are preserved."
> (Lu 5:37-38).

"New wine" needs "new bottles" [leather wineskins] that can stretch and, since "old bottles" could not do so, putting "new wine" in them was an exercise in futility. Likewise, truth that is learned by trusting in the authority of scripture is not compatible with the practice of judging truth according to the teachings of men. Those methods of truth seeking are incompatible, for one desensitizes people to the virtue of God's authority.

"The servant is not greater than his lord; neither he that is sent greater than he that sent him" (Fourth gospel 13:16). So, what men say about God's word cannot be more important than God's word itself. If we have held wrong ideas because we put confidence in men, then we need a new way of deciding what is true on biblical issues.

Chapter 8 – Be Not Deceived

"The fear of the LORD *is* the beginning of knowledge" (Prv 1:7).

A Different Kind of Repentance?

"Repentance" usually brings to mind the idea of giving up misdeeds that are linked to particular sins, and this sort of change *is* necessary. Those who become followers of Jesus have a different standard of behavior than they previously had. However, it is important to note "repentance" is also required when it comes to truth.

A person obviously has to stop resisting the truth in order to receive the truth, yet few think of this in terms of "repentance." Still, scripture talks about "repentance to the acknowledging of the truth" (2 Tm 2:25). So we need to think in those terms if we want to train ourselves to think and speak biblically.

It turns out "repentance to the acknowledging of the truth" is a gift from God. Paul told Timothy how proper instruction might bring about this change in people who "oppose themselves." We learn this from an admonition found in 2 Timothy 2:24-25:

"The servant of the Lord must not strive; but be gentle unto all *men*, apt to teach, patient, in meekness **instructing those that oppose themselves; if God peradventure will give them repentance to the acknowledging of the truth.**"

What does it mean for people to "oppose themselves?" The phrase makes perfect sense, and it identifies the real problem. No one says they want to believe a lie; they tell themselves they want the truth. Thus when people resist the truth, they are opposing what they *claim* they want. The same thing occurs when a person holds contradictory beliefs, for people who believe mutually exclusive ideas are engaged in thinking which opposes itself. The people whom Elijah rebuked for worshipping both the LORD and Baal had relied on this sort of thinking. The practice of self-contradictory thinking was also rebuked by Jesus when he condemned those religious leaders who claimed to respect God's word even while they refused to submit to its authority (Mt 23:15, Mk 7:6-13, et al.).

Earlier we considered the deception in the church in Laodicea and the New Testament has many other examples of faulty thinking both in the church and outside of it. Those "who changed the truth of God into a lie" are at one end of the spectrum and you can read about them in Romans 1:21-26. In the church, the most striking instance of halting "between two opinions" is probably the one rebuked by Paul and Sosthenes in 1 Corinthians 15:12-13:

> "If Christ be preached that he rose from the dead, how say some among you that there is no resurrection of the dead? But if there be no resurrection of the dead, then is Christ not risen."

As this points out, belief in a Christ who "rose from the dead" is not compatible with the idea of "no resurrection of the dead." Those ideas contradict each other, so they cannot both be true. The problem was the willingness of the Corinthians to tolerate error. Their method of assessing truth on biblical issues was flawed because it led them to assume it was reasonable to take an *'agree to disagree'* approach on matters of truth (i.e., they tolerated mutually exclusive ideas and they claimed to respect the truth at the same time). Those who said they followed Jesus had sacrificed the truth for the sake of inclusiveness. However, respect is not shown for the truth when contradictory ideas are considered to be equally valid.

Jesus said, "To this end was I born, and for this cause came I into the world, that I should bear witness unto the truth. Every one that is of the truth heareth my voice" (Fourth gospel 18:37). The link between Jesus and the truth is unbreakable, so Jesus cannot be honored when truth and falsehood are treated as equals!

Followers of Jesus need to respect the truth. 1 Corinthians 15:12-58 made this point to the Corinthians. Those who "oppose themselves" are being unreasonable, so they need to repent of this way of thinking (just as Naaman the leper had to repent of his unreasonable mindset before he could get the blessing of God [as was shown in the earlier discussion of 2 Kings 5:9-14]). The Corinthians were rebuked for not being reasonable, because one cannot respect Jesus who "rose from the dead" and also respect those who say there is "no resurrection of the dead," for this *disrespects* the truth and the authority of scripture.

Divided Loyalties

Is there ever a good reason to reject truth? If not, then no one who respects God's word should ever turn a blind eye to facts in scripture that challenge their view on an issue. Still, some who say they believe scripture are able to come up with high-sounding excuses when they want to resist biblical correction. The religious leaders of Jesus' day did this, and people today still do this. Nevertheless, such behavior certainly does not evidence a love of the truth.

In Hebrews this was said three times: "Today if ye will hear his voice, harden not your hearts" (Heb 3:7-8 & 15, 4:7). Also Jesus said, "My sheep hear my voice, and I know them, and they follow me" (Fourth gospel 10:27). Since "all scripture *is* given by inspiration of God" (2 Tm 3:16) and Jesus spoke the words of God (Fourth gospel 8:28, et al.), those who desire to follow Jesus need to go where the biblical evidence leads.

Can man's response justify God?

"All the people that heard *him* [John the Baptist], and the publicans, **justified God**, being baptized with the baptism of John. But the Pharisees and lawyers rejected the counsel of God against themselves, being not baptized of him" (Lk 7:29-30).

Thus, a right response to the authority of God results in God being "justified." It does so because, in order to receive correction, we must admit we were wrong and submit to God's standard of what is right and true. Conversely, those who will not submit to God's word always find a way to convince themselves they were justified in doing so.

Luke 7:29-30 contrasts two responses to God's authority. When John spoke the word of God, some submitted to its authority and others "rejected the counsel of God." Notice the education the scholars and religious experts had received did not lead them to receive correction! For them to admit they needed correction would call into question the training which led them to be deceived and the beliefs of those who held the same view. This is why our prior training or group affiliations may lead us to resist correction, as can allegiances we may have to a pastor, group, or set of beliefs.

Loyalty can be a good quality. Yet, loyalty to a teacher or group could create a prejudice against the truth if the teacher or group promotes an idea which is not taught by God's word. It is natural for people to associate with those who think like them. However, if we get our cues on what to believe from the people we follow or associate with, then we are not taking our cues from the word of God.

Important? Who Says So?

Some people think resisting the authority of God's word on matters they consider to be little issues is no big deal. Actually it is a big deal because those who do so are, in effect, saying the word of God only has authority when they say it does. If people can give themselves permission to ignore any point in God's word, then they are not under its authority; rather they have usurped authority over it.

People can always come up with an excuse for ignoring something in God's word: 'it is a minor issue,' 'this issue is not worth dividing over,' etc. Nevertheless, those who say an issue is minor or unimportant in order to justify their resistance to truth are doing the same thing the religious leaders did when they justified their resistance to Jesus and John the Baptist (cf. Lk 7:28-35).

Scripture does teach some matters <u>are</u> more important than others. For example, Jesus discussed "the first and great commandment" (Mt 22:38) and he went on to say, "And the second is like unto it" (Mt 22:39). So, we know one came ahead of the other. The difference is this; scripture gets to make this call, not us.

Jesus once said, "Woe unto you, scribes and Pharisees, hypocrites! for ye pay tithe of mint and anise and cumin, and have omitted the **weightier** *matters* of the law, judgment, mercy, and faith: these ought ye to have done, and not to leave the other undone" (Mt 23:23). Jesus and the scholars did not weigh things the same way. Those leaders claimed to value the law, yet in their opinion, "judgment, mercy, and faith" were not as important as the "tithe." If they had said, 'those are minor issues, the tithe is the main thing' would this have made it so? No, because the opinions of men are not the measure of what issues are "weightier."

"Judgment, mercy, and faith" did not suddenly become the "weightier *matters* of the law" when Jesus rebuked the scribes and Pharisees on this issue. Scripture already established this fact. However, Jesus did confront them about their practice of letting their own opinion be the measure of truth. Even if a person correctly identifies the more important issues, it is wrong to ignore lesser issues – for in regard to the less weighty matters Jesus said, "these ought ye to have done."

People are fooling themselves if they claim to respect God's word on issues they deem to be 'essential' or 'major' while they ignore what it says on matters they deem to be 'secondary' or 'minor.' The experts in Jesus' day misjudged him because their judgment was based on their own opinion and not God's word (Mt 12:2 & 10, et al.). Men today who decide what is important or not important based on their own opinion are making the same mistake.

A Substitute Authority

Teaching the word of God faithfully is not done by urging people to put confidence in men. Citing the beliefs of some scholar or group as a way to convince others to adopt a particular belief or viewpoint is not a method that is in line with counsel of God's word.

When we are taught to rely on the beliefs of a man or group, we are wrongly taught **how** to judge what is true. If a man argues, *'you should believe 'x' is true because it is what so-and-so believes,'* is he leading people to trust in the authority of God's word? No. However if he says, *'so-and-so has presented biblical evidence that can prove 'x' is true,'* then he properly acknowledges the work being referenced while he also upholds the authority of God's word.

The issue is what authority is cited and how is the data to be viewed. Should people assume the Bible says what the experts say it says, or should every belief be subject to biblical scrutiny (no matter who said it or how many people believe it)? Anyone can make mistakes, so focusing on scripture keeps us under the authority of God's word.

Choosing Your Measure of Truth

"When ye received the word of God which ye heard of us, ye received *it* not *as* the word of men, but as it is in truth, the word of God, which effectually worketh also in you that believe" (1 Th 2:13). This was written to the brethren in Thessalonica, and earlier we noted the distinction between the word of men and the word of God that is highlighted in this verse. Focusing on this distinction, and being diligent not to let the teachings of men substitute for the authority of God's word, is the key to a better Bible study method.

The practice of regarding God's word as the sole measure of truth on biblical issues was modeled in the case studies. You saw the results. If those results are superior, then relying on the teachings of men is shown to be an inferior method (just as scripture always said), and every teaching must be put to the test of scripture. An effort to subject everything to biblical scrutiny cannot guarantee we will always do so accurately. Still, it upholds scripture as the test of truth and it will keep our pursuit of knowledge grounded in "the fear of the LORD" (Prv 1:7). A scale measures weight, not length. Likewise, the method we use to assess truth on biblical issues must be appropriate to the task. If we rely on the teachings of men to tell us what is true, then we are using a method of assessing truth which is not up to the task.

Study "as to the Lord"

- "Whatsoever ye do in word or deed, do all in the name of the Lord Jesus"(Col 3:17);
- "Whatsoever ye do, do it heartily, as to the Lord, and not unto men" (Col 3:23).

What would happen if we applied the admonition of those verses to the study of God's word? It would remind us our approach to scripture should please the Lord.

The traditions of men promise a shortcut to the truth and some say we should give tradition 'the benefit of the doubt,' but Jesus never encouraged this, nor did his apostles. Instead, they pointed people to the scriptures, and in doing so they showed us the proper method of contending for biblical truth. They never said tradition should be given the benefit of the doubt, neither did they pretend the traditions of men were a good starting point.

If all the truths in God's word have already been discovered by men who are smarter than we are, then why read the Bible? If the scholars can tell us what is true, why not just read them? After all, if we read scripture we might misunderstand it, but if we follow the experts then it will insure we know the truth, right? No! This sort of thinking was promoted by the scholars in Jesus' day and Jesus rebuked them for doing so, most notably in Matthew 15:14 where he described them "blind leaders of the blind." In the verse he went on to say, "if the blind lead the blind, both shall fall into the ditch" (Mt 15:14), so the followers of blind leaders will end up in the same place as the ones they have chosen to follow. Note *they put themselves in that situation* by their choice of who they follow. Is there any hope for them? Yes. It occurs when truth reveals something is amiss. It is the moment when they "fall into the ditch" and the experience, while not pleasant, does call attention to a problem.

God's Wake-up Call

If we have a "fall into the ditch" moment, we should thank God for the wake-up call. For example, if a preacher says, *'Jesus will return on April 1st,'* what of those who assume this is true because they put confidence in that man? If April 2nd arrives and Jesus has not come, then it is their "fall into the ditch" moment. The facts prove they were deceived. The question is, how will they respond to the evidence?

When truth confronts those who have been deceived, some will find a reason to ignore the truth ('it does not matter,' 'it's a minor issue,' etc.) and continue on down the road of error. Others will acknowledge they were deceived, but if they think it is all about one issue (such as date setting in the foregoing example), then they failed to realize their method of assessing truth on biblical issues is what has to change. They will go on practicing the blind following the blind method even if they start following a different man or group. What they need to do is repent of the practice of putting confidence in man. Being confronted with evidence that shows we have been deceived is never going to boost our ego. It does, however, give us an opportunity to grow.

When corrected, we should ponder what caused us to be deceived on that issue. This takes more effort, but if we change our method and lessen the likelihood of deception, then the effort is worthwhile. Furthermore, "Whatsoever ye do, do it heartily, as to the Lord" (Col 3:23) urges us to go the extra mile, and this surely applies to the work we do as we seek to grow in grace and in the knowledge of our Lord and Savior Jesus Christ.

Proper Attribution

This book is not saying it is wrong to ever quote the words of a man, for scripture tells us to give "honor to whom honor" is due (cf. Rom 13:7). It would be wrong *not* to give proper attribution to a person when their research has opened our eyes to something in God's word. Moreover, if we then share those insights with others, we need to be honest and credit person 'x' or book 'y' for teaching us those things. Crediting a resource that provides biblical insights is good because:

(A) scripture indicates it is the right thing to do (Lu 6:31, et al.),
(B) it lets others know where they can get more details on the subject, and
(C) those with whom we share the material can give it further scrutiny, since it is always possible for us to miss something.

If identifying the person or book which teaches us an insight is the right thing to do, then what is the problem with quoting the teachings of men? Scripture is the measure that distinguishes a good method from a bad one. Consider a time when Jesus was confronted by some of the scholars of his day; "The Pharisees and scribes asked him, Why walk not thy disciples according to the tradition of the elders?" (Mk 7:5). What standard did they use to judge the disciples of Jesus? What authority did those scholars cite? It was not God's word, it was "the tradition of the elders!" The teachings of men had replaced the word of God as their measure of right and wrong.

Mark 7:6-7 tells us how Jesus responded to their use of that standard:

"He answered and said unto them, Well hath Esaias prophesied of you hypocrites, as it is written, This people honoreth me with *their* lips, but their heart is far from me. Howbeit in vain do they worship me, teaching *for* doctrines the commandments of men."

He identified the bait and switch of those religious leaders. They said they stood for the truth of God, when they were actually "teaching *for* doctrines the commandments of men" (Mk 7:7).

"The commandments of men" were taught as "doctrines" by those religious leaders. They were promoting a substitute authority over (or in addition to) God's word, and *their desire to cling to their traditions is what led them to do so.* We know this because Jesus identified their self-interested motive when he told them:

(A) "Laying aside the commandment of God, ye hold the tradition of men" (Mk 7:8); and,

(B) "ye reject the commandment of God, **that ye may keep your own tradition**" (Mk 7:9).

Their regard for the authority of men is what led them to trample on the word of God! They had to choose one or the other, since "No man can serve two masters" (Mt 6:24). They judged right and wrong by their substitute measure, and this led Jesus to say they were "making the word of God of none effect" – "through" their "tradition" (Mk 7:13).

When the teachings of men have become our measure of what is true and right, then we are doing the same thing they did and we make God's word ineffective in the same way.

Quoting Men While Honoring God

Clearly, there is no problem with saying, Isaiah said 'x' or Job said 'y;' it was done in scripture. This tells others where a particular teaching can be found. In the same way, crediting a person or book that has helped us to see the truth is not a problem. The problem comes when non-Bible sources are cited as if they are authoritative, because this encourages people to put confidence in those sources.

Citing non-Bible sources and naming proponents of an idea is a tactic some people use to sell an idea to others. This is not the same thing as merely identifying a resource that provides insight on some issue. Most teachers promote ideas they believe are true, and they do so by quoting men who agree with them. (If they quote an opposing view, they will emphasize what is wrong with it.) People make a mistake when they think an idea is true because it is what their preacher and his sources believe. The opinions of men are not the measure of truth on biblical issues. "Forever, O LORD, thy word is settled in heaven" (Ps 119:89) and "O LORD: give me understanding according to thy word" (Ps 119:169) are just two of many passages that let us know God's word is the measure of truth.

If we say our beliefs are biblical, then this claim makes scripture the judge of our beliefs. When a person's beliefs are contrary to scripture on any issue, then scripture is not their authority on that issue.

The Antidote for Error

Paul gave Timothy this warning regarding deception, "Evil men and seducers shall wax worse and worse, deceiving, and being deceived" (2 Tm 3:13). Then he added this:

> "But continue thou in the things which thou hast learned and hast been assured of, knowing of whom thou hast learned them; And that from a child thou hast known the holy scriptures, which are able to make thee wise unto salvation through faith which is in Christ Jesus" (2 Tm 3:14-15).

Would Timothy have thought the words "knowing of whom thou hast learned them" referred to some human teacher? Should we assume this referred to Timothy's mother or grandmother because earlier in the letter Paul wrote, "I call to remembrance the unfeigned faith that is in thee, which dwelt first in thy grandmother Lois, and thy mother Eunice" (2 Tm 1:5)? Lois, Eunice and Paul all taught Timothy. However, if Timothy had received that teaching "not as the word of men, but as it is in truth, the word of God" (as the Thessalonians had done (cf. 1 Th 2:13)), then he learned those things from God. Jesus cited this prophecy, "they shall be all taught of God" (Fourth gospel 6:45) and if those words refer to people who rightly receive "the word of God," then this would surely include Timothy.

Paul told Timothy, "the holy scriptures" had the ability to make him "wise unto salvation" (2 Tm 3:15) and this fits with the results described in 1 Thessalonians 2:13 ("effectually worketh also in you that believe"). Those who faithfully delivered God's word to Timothy played a role, but what made him "wise unto salvation" was "the holy scriptures." Moreover, that result is linked to the source of scripture by this verse: "All scripture is given by inspiration of God" (2 Tm 3:16).

Timothy was told:

> "**Preach the word**; be instant in season, out of season; reprove, rebuke, exhort with all longsuffering and doctrine. For the time will come when they will not endure sound doctrine; but after their own lusts shall they heap to themselves teachers, having itching ears; and they shall turn away *their* ears from the truth, and shall be turned unto fables" (2 Tm 4:2-4).

Truth is the antidote for error. Paul told Timothy to "preach the word" consistently, because if people "will not endure sound doctrine," then at some point they will turn away from the soundness of scripture until they repent.

The phrase "the time will come" let Timothy know his audience would not always be open to the truth. At an individual level this is the point when people turn a blind eye to evidence and begin resisting truth because it makes them feel uncomfortable. They no longer welcome the reproof and rebuke that comes with "sound doctrine." Instead, they listen to men who make them feel justified while they "turn away *their* ears from the truth." This way they can do what they desire while they salve their conscience by pretending their teachers give them a reason to ignore the truth.

"A fool despiseth his father's instruction: but he that regardeth reproof is prudent" (Prv 15:5). We need to invite God's instruction, not resist it. Yet, "Today if ye will hear his voice, harden not your hearts" (Heb 3:7-8 & 15, 4:7) was a warning to the "holy brethren" (Heb 3:1). This lets us know the "holy brethren" may be tempted to resist the "doctrine," "reproof," "correction," and "instruction in righteousness" (2 Tm 3:16) that comes from God's word – and there is no reason to believe the followers of Jesus in our day are immune from this temptation. On the contrary, this temptation may be even greater in the Internet age.

Today, people can easily find teachers who will tell them what they want to hear. Now people can "turn away *their* ears from the truth" and "be turned unto fables" in only a few clicks. The joke says, *'it must be true because it was on the Internet.'* However, when people think something must be true if a famous preacher said it or because they read it in a book (or in the notes of men that are added to the words of scripture in many Bibles), then they are making the same mistake; i.e., they are putting confidence in a source that is not always reliable.

<u>Taught by God?</u>

Jesus once said, "I thank thee, O Father, Lord of heaven and earth, because thou hast hid these things from the wise and prudent, and hast revealed them unto babes" (Mt 11:25, Lk 10:21). Unless God did this only back then, we cannot assume being "wise and prudent" makes a man or group of men more likely to have the truth. So, it would be a mistake to assume "wise and prudent" men understand God's word, or to think it is a good idea to trust "wise and prudent" men to tell us how we should go about learning what is taught by God in scripture.

We learn best when God is teaching us! While this may sound strange to us, the brethren in Ephesus may have reacted the same way when they first read the words: "If so be that ye have heard him [God], and have been taught by him" (Eph 4:21). [References to "God" in verses 18 and 24 confirm the word "him" in verse 21 refers to God.] The verse goes on to say, "as the truth is in Jesus," so this is *what* they learned. Nevertheless, the one who <u>did</u> the teaching was also identified – they had "**heard him** [God]" and "been **taught by him.**" Moreover, since those words were written "to the faithful in Christ Jesus" (Eph 1:1), they are surely still relevant for the followers of Jesus today.

<u>If God's word teaches you something, then who taught you</u>? Since God is the source of scripture, if you have been taught by God's word, then you have been taught by God. This ties into a prophecy that was quoted by Jesus: "It is written in the prophets, And they shall be all taught of God" (Fourth gospel 6:45). In that passage he went on to explain those words and he made this clear – "taught of God" did not refer to being taught *about* God, rather, they meant being taught **by** God.

<u>"Be Renewed"</u>

Right after Ephesians 4:21 is a description of the response that ought to result from being taught by God:

"That ye put off concerning the former conversation the old man, which is corrupt according to the deceitful lusts; And be renewed in the spirit of your mind; And that ye put on the new man, which after God is created in righteousness and true holiness" (Eph 4:22-24).

How can one "be renewed" in accord with the foregoing admonition? In the letter to the Ephesians it also says, Christ "loved the church, and gave himself for it; that he might sanctify and cleanse it with **the washing of water by the word**" (Eph 5:26).

Unless the teachings of men can substitute for "the word" and have the same "washing" effect, then there is the problem. The cleansing effect of the word of God will be undermined or made void every time the teachings of men are promoted as a substitute authority. Another work of "the word" was noted when the brethren were told the Father had begotten them "with the word of truth" (Jas 1:18), or as 1 Peter 1:23 put it, "Being born again, not of corruptible seed, but of incorruptible, by the word of God, which liveth and abideth for ever." If we want the results "the word of truth" is said to produce, then we dare not assume the teachings of men can serve as a stand-in for "the word of God."

"Thy Word is Truth"

Not everyone has a Bible or the ability to read, let alone access to the Internet which lets people utilize a wide array of free Bible study tools. Those of us who have those things need to thank God for them, and one way we can show our gratitude is to make a diligent effort to let scripture be a lamp to our feet and a light to our path. Today the words "Unto whomsoever much is given, of him shall be much required" (Lk 12:48) must be weighed in light of the unique resources available to us in this age.

Once when Jesus prayed for his followers, he asked the Father to "Sanctify them **through thy truth**: thy word is truth" (Fourth gospel 17:17). In the prayer he also said: "Neither pray I for these alone, but for them also which shall believe on me through their word" (Fourth gospel 17:20). "Thy word is truth" identifies a sure measure on biblical issues and we need to respect this standard because the "truth" that comes via God's word is what changes (i.e., sanctifies) the followers of Jesus.

Men will raise other measures of truth, such as when "the chief priests and Pharisees" raised this question about Jesus: "Have any of the rulers or of the Pharisees believed on him?" (Fourth gospel 7:48) Implicit in their question is the idea that the beliefs of the religious leaders are the measure of what is true. It also implies only a fool would disagree with all of those highly intelligent men. No one wants to be the target of ridicule, so such questions are used to bully people into falling in line and lead them to conform their views to the beliefs of other men.

"Foolish and unlearned questions avoid, knowing that they do gender strifes" (2 Tm 2:23). In order to obey this counsel we must be able to tell what questions qualify as "foolish and unlearned." Does this describe, for example, the question, "Have any of the rulers or of the Pharisees believed on him?" If so, then such questions should not intimidate us or be answered, for they promote a false view that must be rejected.

Titus 3:9 says "avoid foolish questions" for "they are unprofitable and vain." As has been shown, the opinions of men about the importance of the tithe led men to disrespect scripture's own standard as to how one could determine what the "weightier" issues were. In addition, we saw how the religious leaders cited their beliefs as the measure of truth and how they pulled a bait and switch by "teaching for doctrines the commandments of men" (Mt 15:9, Mk 7:7). This can also be done through questions that seed false implications. (A crafty question, like a false statement, can lead one to be deceived and we see this in the question which was posed by "the serpent" to "the woman"(Gen 3:1).)

Wise? By What Standard?

Jesus said, "whosoever heareth these sayings of mine, and doeth them, I will liken him unto a wise man, which built his house upon a rock" (Mt 7:24). Thus, we must define godly wisdom in terms of hearing and doing the words of Jesus.

1 Corinthians 3:20 says, "The Lord knoweth the thoughts of the wise, that they are vain." Obviously, this is not referring to people like the "wise man, which built his house upon a rock." By what standard do we define the word "wise?" "The wisdom of this world is foolishness with God" (1 Cor 3:19), so what some people consider to be "wisdom" is the exact opposite in God's eyes. If we want to employ godly wisdom, we need to use the right measure when making judgments.

After Jesus said the "wise man" built "upon a rock," he talked about those who are "foolish" – "every one that heareth these sayings of mine, and doeth them not, shall be likened unto a foolish man, which built his house upon the sand" (Mt 7:26). The "foolish man" *thinks* what he is doing is fine, but this is because he is using a wrong measure. "The way of a fool *is* right in his own eyes: but he that hearkeneth unto counsel *is* wise" (Prv 12:15). Thus, foolish thinking is self-justifying.

Isaiah 5:21 says, "Woe unto *them that are* wise in their own eyes, and prudent in their own sight!" This kind of self-affirming, peer-reviewed thinking was practiced by all of the various groups of religious experts in Jesus' day. The intellectual standard of this world is based on men "measuring themselves by themselves, and comparing themselves among themselves," but scripture tells us those who use this method "are not wise" (2 Cor 10:12). We are "not wise" to be judging our beliefs by measuring them according to the beliefs of others.

Since "The fear of the LORD is the beginning of wisdom" (Ps 111:10, Prv 9:10), "The fear of the LORD is the beginning of knowledge" (Prv 1:7), and "The fear of the LORD *tendeth* to life" (Prv 19:23), we need to let scripture be our measure of "wisdom," not the teachings of men.

Focus on the Reward

"God *is* not unrighteous to forget your work and labor of love, which ye have shewed toward his name" is the amazing encouragement we find in Hebrews 6:10. This was not written to a specific individual, but to the "beloved" (Heb 6:9), and the striking thing to realize is how this lines up with the principle of rewards that is emphasized in scripture.

Never forget: "He that cometh to God must believe *that* he is, and that he is a rewarder of them that diligently seek him" (Heb 11:6). It is easy to see why a man cannot come to God unless he believes God "is." But the other condition is not often considered; <u>to come to God a man must believe God is "a rewarder of them that diligently seek him."</u> So, focusing on this reward is of utmost importance!

What made Moses different? It was a proper esteem for the rewards of God – "Esteeming the reproach of Christ greater riches than the treasures in Egypt: for he [Moses] had respect unto the recompense of the reward" (Heb 11:26). The earthly "treasures in Egypt" were not the only game in town. Moses saw the "greater riches" that came with "the recompense of the reward" and he, rightly, valued this more.

Jesus talked about treasure more than once. In this passage he emphasized the importance of where a person's treasure is located:

"Lay not up for yourselves treasures upon earth, **where** moth and rust doth corrupt, and **where** thieves break through and steal: But lay up for yourselves treasures in heaven, **where** neither moth nor rust doth corrupt, and **where** thieves do not break through nor steal: For **where** your treasure is, there will your heart be also" (Mt 6:19-21).

Moses "had respect unto the recompense of the reward," so this is where his treasure was. Those who come to God "must believe *that* he [God] is, and that he is a rewarder of them that diligently seek him" (Heb 11:6). Even Jesus looked forward to a reward: "Jesus the author and finisher of *our* faith; who for the joy that was set before him endured the cross" (Heb 12:2). Those words give us a look into the mind of Jesus and his regard for the reward. Jesus "endured the cross" **because** he esteemed "the joy that was set before him," and this is the type of mindset his followers should also seek to have (cf. Phi 2:5).

The Secret to Success

"By humility *and* the fear of the LORD *are* riches, and honor, and life" (Prv 22:4). There you go! Still, two things are true:

(A) scripture is "profitable for doctrine, for reproof, for correction, for instruction in righteousness" (2 Tm 3:16), but to obtain those profits we must submit to the authority of God's word, and
(B) those who only see "riches, and honor, and life" in terms of this world's wisdom have not yet let "the fear of the LORD" be the deciding factor in determining their measure of truth.

The ultimate manifestation of "humility" and "the fear of the LORD" was Jesus. Did he attain "riches, and honor, and life?" What scripture says about the resurrection and the life to come teaches us how to answer this. The LORD said, "let him that glorieth glory in this, that he understandeth and knoweth me" (Jer 9:24). But all the time and effort spent on teaching people the world's measure of wisdom is not what leads people to the knowledge this verse is talking about. Just as with the word "wisdom," we must let scripture's use of words teach us how to rightly understand its use of the words, "riches," "honor," "life," etc.

"The fear of the LORD" should lead one to treat the word of God more diligently than those who want others to tell them what the Bible says (so they do not have to read it). Scripture lets us know being taught about God is not the same as being taught by God, so it makes sense for us to spend as much time as we can in God's word. Many people like to say, 'the gospel is the most important thing.' Yet, if the gospel is not taught "according to the scriptures" (1 Cor 15:3-4), then the gospel **of** scripture is not being taught! This holds true for teaching on prayer, worship, and all other biblical issues. The diligent study of God's word can produce much fruit if "the fear of the LORD" is our starting point and it is what determines how we approach the word of God.

<u>Looking Back and Going Forward</u>

For your consideration, here is a review of some key points that were made earlier. It is hoped this will help as you go forward in applying a better Bible study method in your ongoing study of God's word:

- If we conform to God's word, we are better off. So, we should strive to accurately reflect the word of God when we speak and think on biblical issues. Our method of assessing truth needs to conform to the whole counsel of God if it is going to consistently produce results that honor God.
- The counsel of scripture can make us less likely to fall prey to false assumptions. If we improve our Bible study method, then we will reap the benefits from that point onward.
- Naaman changed and gave heed to the words of truth which he had initially ignored (cf. 2 Kgs 5:9-14). In the same way, we are obliged to change when a belief of ours is found to be contrary to God's word. If scripture is inspired by God, then it is unreasonable to hold onto a belief when scripture proves that belief is not biblical.
- A method of assessing truth which leads someone to accept a false view in one area, will most likely have the same effect when it comes to other Bible passages.

- Psalm 138:2 says this about the LORD, "thou has magnified thy word above all thy name." Therefore, we need to reject beliefs which are contrary to scripture if we want to honor the word of the LORD.
- Religious groups and teachers often urge people to rely on the teachings of men. Conversely, Jesus spent a lot of time refuting ideas that were believed and promoted by those who put confidence in man, and other writers of scripture also did likewise in their day. When an idea is supposed to be biblical but people have to use non-Bible sources to justify the idea, then it makes sense for us to be cautious.
- Teachers sometimes quote the belief of some man or group and act as if this proves the belief is true. But if God's word is the measure of truth on biblical issues, then the opinions of men cannot substitute for this standard on any issue.
- **Can men convey the meaning of scripture better than the words of scripture itself?** If not, then the word of God needs to be our measure of truth, not the traditions of men.

"Be Not Deceived"

As was noted earlier, the words "be not deceived" appear in several verses. "Be not deceived; God is not mocked: for whatsoever a man soweth, that shall he also reap" (Gal 6:7) is likely the most well-known of those. [Notice how this idea parallels what Jesus said in Mark 4:24, "with what measure ye mete, it shall be measured to you."] Consider the difference it would make if we kept Galatians 6:7 in mind when we choose whether to:

(A) trust in the LORD and prove all things, or
(B) put confidence in man and lean on our own understanding.

The passage in Galatians 6 goes on to say:

"he that soweth to his flesh shall of the flesh reap corruption; but he that soweth to the Spirit shall of the Spirit reap life everlasting. And let us not be weary in well-doing: for in due season we shall reap, if we faint not. As we have therefore opportunity, let us do good unto all *men*, especially unto them who are of the household of faith" (Gal 6:8-10).

The words "especially unto them who are of the household of faith" put a special emphasis on doing good to members of "the household of faith." Therefore, let us consider how this applies in light of the truth God's word has revealed in this study.

The human body was used to teach believers how to view their ties to one another: "Ye are the body of Christ, and members in particular" (1 Cor 12:27, cf. Rom 12:4-5, 1 Cor 12:12-26). Just as the parts of our body work together for the good of the whole, believers must consider how the things they do can impact the health of the body of Christ.

If the Bible study method modeled in this book opened your eyes to truth, then you are obliged to "do good" to "the household of faith" by using this method in your own study of God's word. Then others in the body of Christ benefit from the fruits of your labor, when you share both the method and the insights God teaches you as you continue to search the scriptures.

<u>Be Diligent</u>

Note five verses:

> "For ever, O LORD, thy word is settled in heaven" (Ps 119:89);
> "The entrance of thy words giveth light; it giveth understanding unto the simple" (Ps 119:130);
> "Thy word *is* very pure" (Ps 119:140);
> "Thy word *is* true *from* the beginning" (Ps 119:160);
> "LORD: give me understanding <u>according to thy word</u>" (Ps 119:169).

Verses such as these should fuel our desire to be taught by, and learn from, the word of God. If we are going to let other men tell us what to think on biblical issues, then our understanding will not be according to God's word, but based on what others say about God's word.

When scripture does not teach an idea and yet men teach that idea *as if it were biblical*, there is a huge flaw in their Bible study method. In order to believe an idea is biblical when that idea is contrary to the facts in scripture, a person must be basing their belief on something other than scripture.

Many religious groups routinely teach people to base their beliefs on something other than scripture [see A Better Bible Study Method, Book One for more on this]. Although religious teachers and groups may not *intend to* mislead people, they nevertheless do so whenever they teach people to put confidence in men contrary to the counsel of scripture.

<u>Is it ever wrong to subject our own understanding to biblical scrutiny (or to do the same with every teaching of men)</u>? If not, then we should do so all the time, on every issue!

We are admonished to be vigilant and loyal to the truth of scripture in verses like, "prove all things; hold fast that which is good" (1 Th 5:21), "blessed is that man that maketh the LORD his trust, and respecteth not the proud, nor such as turn aside to lies" (Ps 40:4), and "let God be true, but every man a liar" (Rom 3:4).

Does all of this mean we should avoid teachers, not attend church, turn off Bible teaching programs on the radio, not use commentaries, etc.? No, and this study has not suggested doing any of those things (and anyone who says otherwise is falsely characterizing this work). However, it certainly does mean we should stop following after men and make "the LORD" our trust instead.

People do not need a degree in order to read the Bible or to use a concordance to see how a word was used in scripture. However, if one is going to benefit from biblical correction, then diligence and a willingness to let God's word transform our minds is vital.

Our judgment needs to be consistent with the word of God because the facts in scripture constitute evidence. The other things said herein are merely a discussion of those facts. This book proposed various conclusions based on the evidence and one must subject these ideas to biblical scrutiny to see if they are true, just as we must do whenever we want to determine what is true on any biblical issue.

Contradiction is a warning sign, for it lets us know something is amiss. If something we see in scripture seems contrary to an idea which we have believed, then the word of God is calling us to take another look at our basis for that belief. Of course, we might find out we had merely misconstrued one or more verses and there really is no contradiction. However, being corrected either way would contribute to our growth.

2 Peter 3:18 urges believers to "grow in grace, and *in* the knowledge of our Lord and Savior Jesus Christ." This change does not happen apart from truth.

Those who love the truth should never be intimidated or impressed by men who cite other men in order to justify their teaching because Proverbs 29:25 says, "The fear of man bringeth a snare: but **whoso putteth his trust in the LORD shall be safe.**"

Those who "trust in the LORD" will "be safe," not those who trust in the teachings of men. This is why we need to be diligent to distinguish between those two different sources of information and, hopefully, this book will provoke people to get in the habit of doing so.

Let God's Word Change You

Consider what was said about "the LORD" in Psalm 138:2, "thou hast magnified thy word above all thy name," in light of what was said by "the LORD" in 1 Samuel 2:30, "**them that honor me I will honor.**" What does this tell us about how we should treat scripture? It tells us if we want "the LORD" to honor us, then we should first honor him, and since "the LORD" wants his word to be magnified, we should realize we honor "the LORD" when we exercise a high regard for his word.

In addressing the "beloved brethren" who had been begotten "with the word of truth" (Jas 1:16 & 18), James said, "be ye doers of the word, and not hearers only, deceiving your own selves" (Jas 1:22). There are at least three things we can learn from this warning:

(A) it is possible for the "brethren" to deceive *themselves*,
(B) just because people initially hear and respond to "the word of truth" does not mean they will continue to do so, and
(C) when people hear the word of God and do not act in accord with what it says, they cause themselves to be deceived.

So, what will we do when God's word challenges us?

Acts 18:24-25 introduces Apollos. He was "mighty in the scriptures," "instructed in the way of the Lord," and "he spake and taught diligently the things of the Lord." Still, even though he was a teacher who was "mighty in the scriptures," it turns out he also needed to be taught.

We have a blind spot when there is something we are not aware of, and this was the case with Apollos. Like anyone in this condition, he was not aware of his ignorance. Scripture tells us he knew "only the baptism of John" (Acts 18:25). This changed when Aquila and Priscilla "took him unto them, and expounded unto him the way of God more perfectly" (Acts 18:26). Aquila and Priscilla are never said to be "mighty in the scriptures" and, yet, Apollos was willing to receive instruction from them. Thereafter, he conformed his teaching to the truth and he went on to tell others what he had learned (cf. Acts 18:27-28).

"The Truth"

Apollos "spake and taught diligently the things of the Lord," yet he was humble enough to accept correction. His willingness to change after he learned the truth is a good example for anyone who wants to honor Jesus. This is because Jesus linked himself to the very idea of "truth" when he said:

"To this end was I born, and for this cause came I into the world, that I should bear witness unto the truth. Every one that is of the truth heareth my voice" (Fourth gospel 18:37).

Moreover, something else Jesus said indicates those who love him will love "the truth," for he said, "I am the way, the truth, and the life" (Fourth gospel 14:6). As was noted earlier, since Jesus identified himself with "the truth," the way people respond to "the truth" says something about the way they would respond to him.

What honors God? Ignoring the truth scripture presents on any issue is not the way to do so. However, exercising a consistent regard for the truth does do so, because God's word "is truth," as Jesus noted when he spoke these words to the Father regarding his disciples: "Sanctify them through thy truth: thy word is truth" (Fourth gospel 17:17). In the same passage, Jesus also said these words to the Father: "this is life eternal, that they might know thee the only true God, and Jesus Christ, whom thou hast sent" (Fourth gospel 17:3). So, respect for the truth is of the utmost importance because eternal life is rooted in truth.

[Not knowing the truth is different than turning a blind eye to it. In the first instance a person is acting in ignorance, but in the latter instance one is kicking against the truth. Resistance to the truth is linked to the hardening of the heart, so this is a risky behavior that scripture surely does discourage. Ignorance can be overcome by truth. But in order for this to occur when it comes to biblical issues one must submit to the authority of God (and this means they must be willing to repent if the testimony of scripture would require them to do so).]

Man's Ways vs. God's Way

Seminaries and teachers often promote the idea that spending time reading the opinions of men is the best way to find out what the Bible has to say. The results in the case studies prove, however, those who want to be taught by God will do better if they focus on the evidence in God's word. The opinions of men are not always wrong, so people can sometimes learn by reading or hearing what others say about a verse or issue. Still, the Bible says, "*It is* better to trust in the LORD than to put confidence in man" (Ps 118:8). So, perhaps the time spent studying the traditions of men would yield better results if it was spent on the study of God's word instead.

Men can be deceived. If men are convinced something is true when it is not true, the things they write or say will promote their false view. They do not intend to deceive others, yet this is what will happen if people trust what they have said or written on that issue. This is why encouraging people to let the opinions of men serve as their measure of truth on biblical issues is dangerous. It trains people to judge the word of God by the teachings of men, when people ought to be doing just the opposite.

Teachers will often attach impressive labels to the non-Bible sources they quote in order to get other people to trust in those sources also. For example, if a teacher says, *'world class Bible scholars believe 'x' is true,'* their audience will usually fall in line and assume 'x' is true and will tend to assume there is no reason to put the idea to the test of scripture. However, urging people to esteem the teachings of men is contrary to the counsel found in verses such as, "let God be true, but every man a liar" (Rom 3:4). In any case, the biblical counsel against putting confidence in men makes no exception for men who are called *'experts'* or *'world class scholars.'*

Unfortunately, some read the admonition, "prove all things" (1 Th 5:21), and assume the best way to do this is to cite the teachings of men on whatever issue is in question. But when the teachings of men are put on a pedestal, then one is acting contrary to the counsel of scripture. We can believe what the Bible says or we can base our belief on what *others say the Bible says.* The problem with the latter method is men can be wrong, and those who let the teachings of men serve as the foundation of beliefs are building on a foundation of shifting sand.

<u>"The Pillar and Ground of the Truth"</u>

The aim of this book is not to tell people what is true on various issues. Rather, it is to show how trusting in God's word to teach us produces better results than letting the beliefs of others define our own beliefs. The results of the case studies show this and the same point is made whenever scripture proves a teaching of men is not biblical.

Like any discussion of biblical issues, what this book says on an issue might be right or it might be wrong. How can one know if what is said is right? Put it to the test. By letting the word of God be the measure of truth on biblical issues, a person can know if an idea in this book or some other book (or even one's own beliefs) are in accord with God's word. This is why the goal has been to encourage the reader to hold to scripture as the measure by which they will assess the truth of every teaching on every biblical issue.

Men who quote other men (*who quoted yet other men*) as their means of convincing people to accept this or that biblical belief are using an unbiblical method. It would be better if Bible teachers used a method that follows the counsel in God's word and rejects the world's method of training people to rely on the opinions of others. If we are going to honor God consistently, then his word needs to be the foundation of our beliefs. If the beliefs of others and teachings in non-Bible sources serve as the basis of our beliefs, then the results will be very different.

1 Timothy 3:15 speaks of "the house of God, which is the church of the living God, the pillar and ground of the truth." Some will carelessly restate this and say, 'the church is the pillar and ground of the truth.' But what happens when people edit God's word like this?

Three entities appear in the verse, "the house of God," "the church," and "the living God." The restated version lifts "the church" out of the middle and ties it to the clause at the end of the statement. So instead of God being "the pillar and ground of the truth," in the edited version "the church" becomes the reference point for the truth. However, this was not the idea Paul was communicating, and we can confirm this by looking at other passages of scripture.

When the church strays from the standard of God's word it runs into trouble and this is made abundantly clear in the Book of Revelation. Read the letters to "the seven churches" and notice how this point is repeatedly made in a series of stern rebukes (cf. Rv 1:4, 11 & 20, 2:1-3:22).

Also, those who 'look to the church to tell them what the truth is' are not honoring God, for they are failing to heed a directive repeated seven times in the Book of Revelation – "He that hath an ear, let him **hear what the Spirit saith** unto the churches" (Rv 2:7, 11, 17 & 29, 3:6, 13 & 22). It does not say to hear what is said by the church. Rather, it directs the one who has "an ear" to hear what is said **to** the churches [plural, not singular] **by** the Spirit (and this upholds the inspired word of God as the measure of truth).

Those who are <u>members of the church can be deceived</u>. Verses like, "O foolish Galatians, who hath bewitched you" (Gal 3:1), and the rebuke to the church in Corinth (1Co 15:12), and the letter sent to the angel of the church of the Laodiceans (Rev 3:14-22), make this clear. Therefore, what is said by those in the church cannot be the measure of truth!

Acting as if what is said by those in the church is the measure of truth puts the words of men above God's word – since the measure of truth in such instances is not what God has said, but what men say about what God has said. These are two very different standards. In one, the source of truth is God. In the other, the conclusions drawn about the word of God by a man or group of men are serving as a substitute source of truth.

By What Standard?

How should we go about determining what is true on biblical matters? This question was raised at the beginning of this book and has been raised throughout this work. By what standard should people judge when they want to separate truth from error?

Many assume the way to know what is true on a biblical issue is to see where men agree on the issue. However, men make mistakes, and can be deceived. So it is unreasonable to think their shared view on a given issue must be correct because they agree with each other.

When you hear or read statements involving biblical issues, pause to ask yourself questions like:

(A) Does the statement reflect what is actually said in scripture?
(B) Would it apply to Jesus and the writers of scripture?

The words "prove all things" (1 Th 5:21) urge an evidence-based method of assessing truth, and this also indicates we should be willing to put our own beliefs to the test.

By what standard can a person know if they are rightly understanding the words in a passage of scripture? Since the words of scripture are inspired by God, <u>our understanding of the words of scripture ought to be shaped by how those words were used by the writers of scripture</u> (and the Case of God's Gift showed how this works).

When we discuss biblical issues our goal should not be to get others to agree with us (because we could be mistaken). But if we focus on what scripture says, then God's living and active word can lead others and/or us to take a fresh look at the issue. It also invites others to put our statements to the test, and if we have strayed from scripture, then they can call our attention to the evidence we have missed so we can be corrected.

Honor God

"The LORD" said, "them that honor me I will honor" (1 Sa 2:30), and those who honor God's word might have the honor of being corrected by it.

When our eyes are opened to a truth showing we have been mistaken on an issue, we need to thank God and figure out what went wrong with our method of assessing truth in that instance.

Jesus said, "Suppose ye that I am come to give peace on earth? I tell you, Nay; but rather **division**" (Lu 12:51), so the consensus of opinion was not going to unite around the truth he presented, and it is wrong to assume "division" is always a bad thing. Moreover, since Jesus caused division, we should not be surprised to see God's word having the same effect in our day.

If we quote scripture to show where men have been deceived and we are accused of *'causing division'* for doing so, does the accusation prove we have done anything wrong? No. Often this charge is raised merely to cut-off discussion, change the subject, and dissuade others from giving the question serious consideration. But if such tactics can lead us to set aside or suppress a truth that is presented in scripture, then we are letting peer pressure turn us away from honoring God.

Just how important is it to respect the authority of God's word from beginning to end? In Luke 16:17 Jesus said, "it is easier for heaven and earth to pass, than one tittle of the law to fail." A few verses later, we read where he ended his teaching on Lazarus and the rich man with the following words, "If they hear not Moses and the prophets, **neither will they be persuaded, though one rose from the dead**" (Lu 16:31). Do you realize the profound implication of this statement?

It lets us know the word of God spoken by "Moses and the prophets" carries the same import as the miracle of one rising from the dead! The reason for this is the authority and power of God is the source of both of those things, so here again scripture highlights the need for a consistent respect for the authority of God.

Drunkenness impairs a person's ability to judge their ability to drive. Similarly, <u>false assumptions impair one's ability to judge their ability to discern what is true</u>.

Those who rely on the teachings of men to be the test of what is true are operating under the influence of a false assumption. In spite of the counsel of scripture, they believe the way to learn biblical truth is to look to the opinions of men. However, they are relying on a method that is not reliable, as the case studies herein have shown.

If we change our method of assessing truth on biblical issues, then it will affect how we view biblical issues from that point on. In the same way, using an evidence-based Bible study method will lead us to see things in scripture which we overlooked or misconstrued when we trusted the teachings of men to tell us what to think on those issues.

When the evidence in God's word can prove we have been wrong on some point, we should not feel bad. Rather, we should be grateful for the correction and enjoy the opportunity to grow in knowledge.

Opinion vs. Evidence

Being persuaded by someone else's conclusions about the evidence is not the same as being persuaded by the evidence itself.

If you are discussing a biblical issue and someone says, *'Here is what I think/my opinion...,'* what should you do? When people tell you what they believe, you will know what they think, but you will not know why. The truth would be better served if we asked people to tell us about the biblical evidence that led them to hold their view. This allows us to weigh the evidence for ourselves and avoid falling into the trap of basing our beliefs on the beliefs of someone else. Whenever we are considering scriptural issues, asking questions like these can help us to focus on what the word of God actually says:

- Where does scripture say that?
- Can you show me that in the Bible?
- What in scripture would lead someone to hold that view?

Those of us who have the word of God have been given a great gift. With that, comes the responsibility to recognize the value of this gift.

Jesus said, "the kingdom of heaven is like unto treasure hid in a field; the which when a man hath found, he hideth, and for joy thereof goeth and selleth all that he hath, and buyeth that field" (Mt 13:44). If the truth communicated by God though scripture is truly a treasure, then how should we respond if God opens our eyes so we see a Bible truth that others had overlooked? Would the "joy" of this insight lead us to react in a way that showed we value the truth above all else? Well it might if we were diligent to heed these words, "Buy the truth, and sell *it* not; *also* wisdom, and instruction, and understanding" (Prv 23:23).

Jesus said, "Thou shalt love the Lord thy God with **all** thy heart, and with **all** thy soul, and with **all** thy mind" (Mt 22:37), and this indicates a 100% commitment should be our goal. The Book of Hebrews rebuked those who were "dull of hearing" (Heb 5:11) and "unskillful in the word of righteousness" (Heb 5:13). Hebrews 5:14 then contrasts them with "those who **by reason of use** have their senses exercised to discern both good and evil" (Heb 5:14). In this verse mature followers of Jesus are identified as those who "have their senses exercised to discern both good and evil," and it says this came about "by reason of use."

The growth that comes from exercising discernment cannot happen when a person relies on other people to do their discerning for them. This is why the case studies offered you the opportunity to exercise your own ability to discern between right and wrong, truth and error. Lord willing, those who did the work now see how they can get better at exercising discernment when it comes to their study of God's word.

"The Word"

How important is a proper understanding of the word of God? "When any one heareth the word of the kingdom, and **understandeth** it **not**, then cometh the wicked one, and catcheth away that which was sown in his heart" (Mt 13:19). Those words indicate a right understanding is necessary for "the word" to take root in those who hear it!

We are told Christ "loved the church, and gave himself for it; that he might sanctify and cleanse it with the washing of water **by the word**" (Eph 5:25-26). Elsewhere, Jesus spoke these words to his disciples: "Now ye are **clean through the word** which I have spoken unto you" (Fourth gospel 15:3).

Exposure to "the word" should have cleansing effect and this aptly describes the change that happens when the evidence in scripture moves a person from error to truth on any issue.

Peter received this warning from heaven, "What God hath cleansed, that call not thou common" (Acts 10:15). If this expresses a principle applicable to any cleansing done by God, then we dare not disrespect the cleansing that is done by "the word."

If God's word exposes people to the truth on an issue and they ignore or trivialize that information in order to cling to their prior ways/views, then the words of Proverbs 26:11 would surely apply in such cases: "As a dog returneth to his vomit, so a fool returneth to his folly."

In addition to cleansing and correction, the word of God can result in other forms of change. Romans 10:17 says, "faith cometh by hearing, and hearing by the word of God." This describes a process of change where the end result of "faith" has its beginnings in "the word of God:"

(A) "the word of God" leads to "hearing," and
(B) that "hearing" subsequently goes on to bring about "faith."

Conversely, however, there is no reason to assume "faith" will result when God's word is disobeyed.

Moreover, the change that occurs when one is "born again" is linked to "the word." This was noted earlier when we considered this verse, "Being born again, not of corruptible seed, but of incorruptible, **by the word of God**" (1 Pt 1:23), and the words, "Of his own will begat he us **with the word of truth**" (Jas 1:18) are further confirmation of this truth. If "the word" is key to birth, growth, cleansing, and correction, then why would any follower of Jesus refuse to submit to the authority of God's word on any issue? Is anything worth the cost of ignoring the evidence in scripture and resisting correction on any issue? No.

Jesus said, "How can ye believe, which receive honor one of another, and seek not the honor that *cometh* from God only?" (Fourth gospel 5:44). Unless those words only applied in Jesus' day, we need to consider the principle they set forth. His words indicate the ability to believe is rooted in or tied to seeking the honor that comes "**from God only**." They had received honor from other men instead of seeking the honor that comes "from God only," and the verse indicates when this occurs it interferes with one's ability to "believe." Those who "**receive honor one of another**" pay a cost for doing so, and the cost is not worth it.

<u>"Grace and Truth"</u>

Since "grace and truth came by Jesus Christ" (Fourth gospel 1:17), both those attributes need to come together in the body of Christ in order for it to accurately represent Jesus. As this book has tried to show, those who uphold God's word as the standard of truth honor God by doing do. But we also need to exhibit grace when we share the truth with those who have been deceived, and we can do this by patiently and persistently directing people to the biblical evidence.

"Grace and truth" go together, so "grace" would not lead us to ignore or accommodate false beliefs in order to make others feel good about themselves. We can "hate every false way" (Ps 119:104 & 128) and still show "grace" to those who are deceived and/or promote falsehood. The way to do so is by "speaking the truth in love" (cf. Eph 4:15).

If you were deceived about something, would you want someone to point you to evidence showing this was the case, or would you want them to leave you in your deception to avoid hurting your feelings and your ego?

If we want people to share the truth with us when we are wrong, then the words "thou shalt love thy neighbor as thyself" (Lv 19:18) tell us how we ought to deal with those who we know are in error.

"Be not deceived; God is not mocked: for whatsoever a man soweth, that shall he also reap" (Gal 6:7). Here is the principle – what happens at the start of a process corresponds to the results that are produced. Moreover, the next verse then says, "For he that soweth to his flesh shall of the flesh reap corruption; but he that soweth to the Spirit shall of the Spirit reap life everlasting" (Gal 6:8). Therefore, those who desire to obtain "life everlasting" need to avoid sowing to the flesh because that will lead to the opposite result.

Biblical Correction is a Test

Proverbs 3:12 says, "whom the LORD loveth he correcteth." Thus, we should not resent biblical correction, rather, it should encourage us. For example, many people read where Jesus said, "I have a baptism to be baptized with; and how am I straitened till it be accomplished" (Lu 12:50) and simply go on to the next verse. But if we let God's word teach us, then it can open our eyes to truths we would otherwise miss – and we might notice Jesus was referring to his future baptism!

Were you aware scripture required this additional baptism of Jesus? Ask most churchgoers about Jesus' baptism and chances are they will talk about the time when John the Baptist baptized Jesus in water and "the Spirit of God" descended upon him "like a dove" (Mt 3:13-16). What they ought to say is, 'Which one?' People tend not to ask this because Jesus' baptism by John is usually presented as 'the' baptism of Jesus (as if it was the only one in scripture), which leads people to assume Jesus had only one baptism. Any teaching on Jesus' baptism that mentions only those things related to his baptism by John will tend to lead people to be blind to the teaching of scripture that proves **Jesus had to have more than one baptism**.

If you were operating under the false assumption that there was only one baptism of Jesus, then the moment Luke 12:50 opens your eyes to the truth, you should thank God for the correction. If you went on to search the scriptures on the topic of baptism, you might find where Jesus asked the sons of Zebedee about a future baptism; "Are ye able to drink of the cup that I shall drink of, and to be baptized with the baptism that I am baptized with?" (Mt 20:22) You might also notice Hebrews 6:2 speaks of "the doctrine of baptisms" – plural. Along with Luke 12:50, this could lead you to ask questions like:

- Has this baptism of Jesus already taken place (and if so, was it at his resurrection or on the cross or at some other time)?
- How many baptisms of Jesus are taught by scripture?
- If he had more than one baptism, would this also hold true for those who are the members of the body of Christ?

Did you think there was only one baptism of Jesus? If so, then change your method of assessing truth on biblical issues and use the method modeled in this book as you seek biblical correction on this matter.

Jesus said, "It is written in the prophets, And they shall be all taught of God" (Fourth gospel 6:45) (and when this was cited earlier it was noted that "**taught of God**" refers to being taught by God, not about God).

Likewise, in 1 John 2:27 we find these words written to those who had received the anointing of God, "ye need not that any man teach you," and it goes on to say, "the same anointing teacheth you of all things." We also find very similar language being used by Jesus when he told his disciples, "the Holy Ghost, whom the Father will send in my name, he shall teach you all things" (Fourth gospel 14:26).

"All scripture *is* given by inspiration of God" (2 Tm 3:16), so it follows that when we are taught by Luke 12:50 or any passage of scripture, then we have been taught by God.

God is not honored when we stubbornly hold on to beliefs which are contrary to God's word. Jesus said, "No man can serve two masters: for either he will hate the one, and love the other; or else he will hold to the one, and despise the other" (Mt 6:24). Interestingly, this parallels how people tend to react when something in scripture does not fit with one of their beliefs: they hate falsehood and love the truth or they will cling to their own understanding and turn a blind eye to any evidence that challenges their view. One of those responses manifests a love of the truth and this is how we must respond if we want to honor God.

The Bible study method modeled herein works because it honors the authority of God, and it trusts God's word to teach us directly. It takes more diligence than letting teachers, commentaries, etc. tell us what others think and adopting their conclusions as our own, but it delivers better results, as the case studies have shown. One final example.

Many think a good tool to use when talking to unbelievers about God is Pascal's Wager, which is typically summed up something like this: *'one should bet on God because if God is not real you lose nothing, since you will have no regrets when you are dead, but if God is real, then you win'*. This argument can impress those who judge based on the wisdom of the world, but put it to the test of scripture and it fails. Paul said, "If in this life only we have hope in Christ, we are of all men most miserable" (1 Cor 15:19). That is not *'if we die believing a lie, we lose nothing'*. Rather, he argued if the promises of God are not true, then we are to be pitied, and we need to tell it like it is, just as he did.

How should we go about determining what is true on biblical matters? We should do so according to the scriptures, on any and every issue. Yet, some will not do so because they do not care to have their beliefs put to the test, and these closing remarks are addressed to them.

Tests were used in scripture to prove what was in a person's heart (Ex 16:4, Du 8:16, Ps 26:2, et al.) and, surely, it is a test for us whenever we must choose between truth and our views/beliefs/traditions.

Jesus warned, "When any one heareth the word of the kingdom, and understandeth _it not_, then cometh the wicked _one_, and catcheth away that which was sown in his heart" (Mt 13:19). Therefore, understanding is critical. Moments later he also said, "he that received seed into the good ground is he that heareth the word, and understandeth _it_; which also beareth fruit" (Mt 13:23). "The word" needs to be understood if it is going to bear "fruit"! Moreover, Paul's reprimand of those who teach while "understanding neither what they say, nor whereof they affirm" (1 Tm 1:7) likewise shows understanding is vital. Still, it is not enough.

If we know the truth, then we must obey it. "O foolish Galatians, who hath bewitched you, that ye should not obey the truth" (Gal 3:1), was a rebuke to those who did not "obey the truth." So, they knew the truth, but they did not conform their thoughts and deeds to that knowledge. Given that scripture says, "rebellion _is as_ the sin of witchcraft, and stubbornness _is as_ iniquity and idolatry" (1Sa 15:23), one can see why the word "bewitched" was linked with their disobedience to the truth.

God wants people "to come unto the knowledge of the truth" (1 Tm 2:4). However, the Bible tells of many who would not do so, such as those who "turn away _their_ ears from the truth" (2 Tm 4:4) or who "believed on" Jesus (Fourth gospel 12:42), but would not acknowledge the truth because "they loved the praise of men more than the praise of God" (Fourth gospel 12:43). Did their response matter? If scripture challenges our view on some issue, does it make a difference how we respond?

Jesus said, "He that is of God heareth God's words" (Fourth gospel 8:47). We should keep this in mind whenever scripture says something that does not line up with our understanding of things, for those moments could be the kind of test Proverbs 17:3 was referring to when it said, "**the LORD trieth the hearts**."

Free eBook versions and printable downloads of this book, answers to frequent questions, links to free Bible software and Bible study tools, along with future biblical case studies as they are released, will be made available online at **ABetterBibleStudyMethod.com**

Postscript

"*It is* better to trust in the LORD than to put confidence in man" (Ps 118:8).

"There is a way which seemeth right unto a man, but the end thereof *are* the ways of death" (Prv 14:12).

"Every way of a man *is* right in his own eyes" (Prv 21:2).

"Every word of God *is* pure: he *is* a shield unto them that put their trust in him. Add thou not unto his words, lest he reprove thee, and thou be found a liar" (Prv 30:5-6).

"Thou shalt not bear false witness" (Mt 19:18).

"Blessed is that man that maketh the LORD his trust, and respecteth not the proud, nor such as turn aside to lies" (Ps 40:4).

"He that trusteth in his own heart is a fool: but whoso walketh wisely, he shall be delivered" (Prv 28:26).

"The fear of the LORD *is* the beginning of knowledge: *but* fools despise wisdom and instruction" (Prv 1:7).

"Hear instruction, and be wise, and refuse it not" (Prv 8:33).

"The ear that heareth the reproof of life abideth among the wise. He that refuseth instruction despiseth his own soul: but he that heareth reproof getteth understanding" (Prv 15:31-32).

"Prove all things; hold fast that which is good" (1 Th 5:21).

"Judge not according to the appearance, but judge righteous judgment" (Fourth gospel 7:24).

"The heart of the righteous studieth to answer" (Prv 15:28).

"The heart of the prudent getteth knowledge; and the ear of the wise seeketh knowledge" (Prv 18:15).

"Trust in the LORD with all thine heart; and lean not unto thine own understanding. In all thy ways acknowledge him, and he shall direct thy paths" (Prv 3:5-6).

"He that is of God heareth God's words." (Fourth gospel 8:47).

Index